MONEY SKILLS FOR YOUNG ADULTS

MONEY SKILLS FOR YOUNG ADULTS

BUILD SMART MONEY SKILLS

CORINTHIA DAVIS

Corinthia Davis
Money Skills for Young Adults

Published by Spines Publishing Platform
ISBN: 979-8-90222-214-9

Spines

CONTENTS

INTRODUCTION

When Hurricane Katrina hit New Orleans in August 2005, everything I had built seemed to wash away overnight. My business, my home, and my sense of security were suddenly gone. But I had one thing that couldn't be taken from me: financial skills. These skills, refined through years of dedication to accounting and financial management, became my beacon of hope. They were the very tools I wielded to rebuild my existence and forge a new path forward. Years of dedication to accounting and numbers became my lifeline. They were the tools I used to rebuild my life and start anew.

This book is about those skills. It's about equipping you, a young adult standing on the brink of your financial future, with the practical tools you need to succeed. We will explore budgeting, saving, and investing in ways that are relatable and actionable. The aim is not just to teach you about money but to help you transform your financial future.

Young adults today face a slew of financial challenges. Student loans loom large, credit scores can be mysterious, and saving for emergencies feels daunting. According to recent surveys, a significant percentage of young adults struggle with managing their debt and understanding financial concepts. This is why financial literacy is more urgent than ever. You need to be equipped to navigate these challenges with confidence.

Let me share a bit of my journey. I started Davis Professional Accounting Services from scratch, without borrowing a dime. It wasn't easy. I built my business one client at a time while also raising my daughter as a single mother. I poured countless hours into my work, driven by a passion for numbers and a determination to succeed. This journey wasn't just about making money; it was about creating a stable future for my family.

My background in accounting and my experiences as a single mother lend credibility to the advice in this book. I've lived through financial ups and downs, and I've learned valuable lessons along the way. I understand what it means to face financial uncertainty and to push through adversity. This book is a culmination of those experiences and insights. My father taught me about saving and investing from an early age. My mom always said I can do hard things and that inspired me to write a book about my knowledge.

As you turn the pages, you'll find a structured guide to money management. We'll start with budgeting because understanding where your money goes is the foundation of financial success. Next, we'll tackle credit management and explore how to build and maintain a healthy credit score. Finally, we'll delve into investing, demystifying the process and showing you how to grow your wealth over time.

But this isn't just about reading; it's about action. I encourage you to take control of your financial destiny. You have the power to change your financial story, and this book will give you the tools to do just that. Whether you're just starting out or looking to improve your current situation, the steps you take now will shape your future.

Expect practical advice, relatable examples, and actionable steps that you can implement right away. This isn't about making you a financial expert overnight; it's about giving you the knowledge and skills to make smarter decisions and achieve financial success.

Let's get started. Your financial future is waiting, and it's time to take the first step.

CHAPTER 1
MASTERING BUDGETING BASICS

The moment I realized the power of effective budgeting was when I was a single mother, trying to stretch every dollar while building my accounting business from the ground up. With limited resources and a child to care for, I learned quickly that every dollar needed a purpose. Each cent had to be accounted for, not just for survival but for growth. Budgeting wasn't merely about cutting costs; it was about setting a foundation for a secure future—a lesson I wish I'd known even earlier. This chapter is designed to guide you through similar realizations, transforming the way you manage money from a daunting task to an empowering tool.

SETTING UP A REALISTIC BUDGET: A STEP-BY-STEP GUIDE

To begin, let's talk about budgeting goals. Think of them as the roadmap to your financial aspirations. Whether it's saving for a short-term goal like a summer road trip or a long-term dream like buying a house, these objectives need to resonate with your personal values. Setting clear, achievable goals gives you direction and motivation. Start by writing down what truly matters to you and what you aim to achieve financially. This isn't just about numbers; it's about aligning your spending with what brings you joy and satisfaction. Setting goals that mean something to you makes the entire budgeting process far more personal and engaging.

Next, let's get into the nitty-gritty of calculating income and expenses. Understanding the difference between your net and gross income is crucial. Your gross income is what you earn before taxes and deductions, while your net income is what you actually take home. Knowing this helps you set more realistic financial goals. Break down your expenses into fixed and variable categories. Fixed expenses are those that don't change monthly, like rent or a car payment, while variable expenses, like groceries and entertainment, can fluctuate. This breakdown allows you to see where your money is going, which is the first step in taking control of it.

Once you've got a handle on your income and expenses, it's time to create a budget framework. One popular method is the "50/30/20 rule," which suggests allocating 50% of your income to needs, 30% to wants, and 20% to savings or paying off debt (SOURCE 1). This gives you a balanced approach to managing money, ensuring that essential costs are covered while still allowing room for enjoyment and future planning. Alternatively, you might consider "zero-based budgeting," where you assign every dollar to a specific purpose until there's nothing left unaccounted for. This method can be particularly effective if you want complete control over your spending habits.

Now, implementing these budgeting practices is where the real work begins. To make your budget stick, it's vital to regularly review and adjust your plan. Holding monthly budget review meetings with yourself or an accountability partner can keep you on track and motivated (SOURCE 3). An accountability partner can provide support, encouragement, and an outside perspective, making it easier to stick to your budget. This practice transforms budgeting from a solitary task into a shared journey, boosting morale and providing the reinforcement needed to achieve your financial goals.

To cement these new habits, consider setting up small milestones and celebrating when you reach them. These milestones act as checkpoints, keeping you motivated and focused on the bigger picture. When you pay off a debt or reach a savings goal, take a moment to acknowledge your achievement. This recognition boosts your confidence and reinforces positive financial behaviors, making budgeting a rewarding rather than a burdensome task. Remember, the journey to financial stability is not a sprint but a marathon, and each step forward is progress.

UNDERSTANDING THE DIFFERENCE: NEEDS VS. WANTS

Understanding the difference between needs and wants is a fundamental step in effective budgeting. Needs are those expenses that are crucial for your survival and well-being. They include rent, groceries, utilities, and healthcare. These are the non-negotiables in life—the expenses that, if neglected, could seriously impact your quality of life. On the other hand, wants are those little luxuries that make life enjoyable but aren't strictly necessary. This could be dining out, that streaming service subscription, or the latest tech gadget. Differentiating between these two categories is vital. It helps you see where your money should go first and where you might be overspending.

To start evaluating your spending habits, take a good look at your bank statements. This is where you'll find the story of your financial life laid bare. Look for patterns. Do you spend more on weekends? Are there recurring charges for things you no longer use or need? Identifying these spending triggers is key to making adjustments. Perhaps it's the after-work coffee runs or the weekend shopping trips that are quietly eating away at your budget. Recognizing these habits is the first step toward change. Once you've spotted the trends, you can begin to shift your behavior and make more intentional choices about where your money goes.

Now, let's talk about adjusting your spending to better align with your financial goals. Start by reducing non-essential purchases. This doesn't mean cutting out all fun, but it does mean making more mindful decisions. If you're saving for a big goal, like a vacation or a new car, redirect funds from wants to savings. For example, instead of going out for dinner, you might choose to cook at home and put the money you would have spent into your savings account. This doesn't just help you save money; it can also be a way to practice discipline and focus on what truly matters to you. By consciously reallocating funds, you're actively working toward your goals.

For those who find managing expenses challenging, consider using budgeting tools to streamline the process. The envelope system is a tried-and-true method where you allocate cash for different spending categories. Once the cash is gone, so is your spending for that category. This method helps to physically limit spending and keeps your budget tangible. If digital solutions are more your style, explore apps and online tools that categorize expenses automatically. By setting up categories within these tools, you can easily track your spending and see where adjustments are needed. These tools provide a visual representation of your financial habits, making it easier to stay accountable and make informed decisions.

PRIORITIZING EXPENSES: NEEDS VS. WANTS

To grasp the distinction between needs and wants is a pivotal first step in crafting a functional budget.

- **Needs** encompass those critical expenses essential for your survival and overall well-being, such as housing, food, utilities, and healthcare. These are the indispensable elements of your financial planning—expenses that, if overlooked, could drastically diminish your quality of life.
- Conversely, **Wants** represent the enjoyable yet non-essential luxuries of life, like dining out, subscriptions to streaming services, or the latest electronic gadgets.

Recognizing the difference between these two categories is crucial, as it illuminates where your financial priorities should lie and identifies potential areas of excessive spending. To begin examining your expenditure patterns, conduct a thorough review of your bank statements.

This exercise lays bare the narrative of your financial habits. Look for spending patterns. Are your expenses higher on weekends? Do you notice recurrent charges for services or items you no longer enjoy or require? Identifying these spending triggers is essential for implementing change. It could be the habitual coffee purchases post-work or frequent weekend shopping sprees subtly draining your budget. Acknowledgment of these patterns marks the initial step towards financial modification.

Once you've identified these trends, you can start to make deliberate choices on how to allocate your funds more wisely. Shifting towards aligning your spending with your financial aspirations involves curtailing non-essential expenditures. This is not to suggest eliminating all forms of enjoyment, but rather adopting a more thoughtful approach to spending.

If you're earmarking funds for significant objectives, like a holiday or a new vehicle, consider diverting money from 'wants' to your savings. Opting to prepare meals at home rather than eating out, for instance, allows you to channel the savings into your financial goals. This strategy not only aids in accumulating savings but also in cultivating financial discipline and keeping your focus on what's truly important to you. By consciously redirecting funds, you're proactively contributing towards achieving your objectives.

For those who find it challenging to manage their expenses, employing budgeting tools can simplify the process significantly. The envelope system, a proven method, involves allocating cash for various spending categories. Once the cash designated for a category is depleted, spending in that category ceases. This approach effectively curbs spending and renders your budget more tangible. If you prefer digital solutions, numerous apps and online tools automatically categorize expenses, facilitating easy tracking and adjustment of your spending. These tools offer a visual breakdown of your financial activities, enhancing your ability to remain accountable and make educated financial decisions.

Exercise: Self-Assessment of Needs vs. Wants

Dedicate some time to listing your monthly expenditures, categorizing them into "Needs" and "Wants". As you classify each expense, critically evaluate why it falls into its respective category. Is it an absolute necessity, or is it something you can do without? This exercise transcends mere cost-cutting; it's about comprehensively understanding your spending habits and ensuring they align with your values and objectives.

Regularly conducting this self-assessment will improve your financial oversight, enabling your money to serve your purposes more effectively. Prioritizing expenses goes beyond mere austerity. It's about gaining clarity and acting with purpose. When you're aware of your needs and wants, you can make decisions with confidence. This allows for occasional indulgences in your wants without remorse, secure in the knowledge that your essential needs are met, and your financial goals are within reach. Achieving this balance is fundamental to fostering a sustainable financial future. A moment to list your monthly expenses. Separate them into two columns: "Needs" and "Wants". As you categorize, ask yourself why each item belongs in its column. Is it truly a necessity, or is it something you could live without? This exercise isn't just about cutting costs. It's about understanding your spending choices and aligning them with your values and goals. By doing this regularly, you'll gain better control over your finances and ensure your money works for you, not against you.

Prioritizing expenses is not about deprivation. It's about clarity and intention. When you know what your needs and wants are, you can make more informed decisions. You can choose to indulge in wants occasionally without guilt, knowing that your needs are covered, and your goals are in sight. This balance is key to a sustainable financial future.

BUDGETING TOOLS AND APPS: CHOOSING THE RIGHT FIT

In today's digital age, budgeting apps have become indispensable tools for managing finances. They offer a level of convenience and efficiency that traditional methods simply cannot match. Among the popular options, Mint stands out for its user-friendly interface and comprehensive features. It allows you to connect all your financial accounts in one place, providing a holistic view of your finances. With automatic categorization of expenses and personalized budgeting tips, Mint is like having a financial advisor in your pocket. Y NAB, or You Need A Budget, takes a different approach. It focuses on proactive budgeting, encouraging you to allocate every dollar to a specific purpose. This app is ideal for those who want to take a hands-on approach to their finances, offering workshops and educational resources to bolster financial literacy. Personal Capital is another powerful tool, especially for those interested in investing. It provides detailed insights into your net worth and investment portfolio, making it a favorite among those looking to build wealth. And then there's Pocket Guard, which simplifies budgeting by showing you how much disposable income you have after accounting for bills and necessities. It's perfect for people who want quick, at-a-glance financial information.

When choosing the right app for your needs, consider the features that matter most to you. If you prefer an intuitive user interface, Mint might be your best bet, with its sleek design and ease of use. For those who need detailed reporting and analytics capabilities, Personal Capital offers in-depth insights that can guide your financial decisions. Y NAB is a great App if you value educational support and want to learn more about budgeting strategies. Each app has its strengths, so think about what aligns with your financial goals and daily habits. Do you need real-time updates or detailed analysis? Would you prefer a simple overview or a comprehensive financial picture? These questions can guide you in selecting an app that complements your lifestyle.

Using digital tools for budgeting offers several advantages over traditional methods. With apps, you get real-time updates on your spending, helping you stay on top of your finances with minimal effort. They automate many tasks, like categorizing expenses and tracking bills, which can save you time and reduce human error. However, there are also drawbacks to consider. Digital methods require sharing your financial data, which raises privacy concerns for some users. In contrast, traditional methods like spreadsheets or paper budgets keep your information offline, reducing the risk of data breaches. Manual entry can also lead to a more profound understanding of your spending habits, as it requires more engagement with your finances. Each method has trade-offs, so it's crucial to weigh them according to your comfort level and priorities.

One of the significant benefits of budgeting apps is their

ability to integrate seamlessly with your financial accounts. By linking your bank accounts and credit cards, these apps can automatically track and categorize your transactions, providing a clear picture of your financial health without the need for manual input. This automation can save you time and ensure accuracy, allowing you to focus on making informed financial decisions. For example, Mint and Personal Capital offer robust integration features, making it easy to manage everything from checking accounts to investment portfolios in one place. On the other hand, if privacy is a primary concern, you might opt for an app that allows manual entry without requiring direct access to your accounts, ensuring your data stays secure.

When selecting a budgeting tool, reflect on your financial habits and needs. Are you someone who enjoys analyzing data and delving into the minutiae of your finances? Or do you prefer a quick overview that allows you to see the big picture without getting bogged down in details? Consider how you interact with technology and what will keep you engaged in maintaining your budget. The right app should feel like a natural extension of your financial management strategy, enhancing your ability to make smart financial choices and achieve your goals. As you explore these tools, remember that the best choice is one that simplifies your life and supports your journey towards financial success.

TRACKING SPENDING HABITS: STAYING ACCOUNTABLE

Monitoring your spending isn't just about creating a budget; it's about ensuring that your budget actually works for you over time. Regular monitoring of expenses is a crucial step in maintaining financial discipline. It's like keeping a diary for your wallet, a daily log that provides insights into where your money is going. By noting down every purchase, no matter how small, you begin to see patterns that were perhaps invisible before. This practice not only helps in sticking to a budget but also in understanding your financial habits. A daily expense log can be a simple notebook or a spreadsheet where each transaction is recorded. At first, it might seem tedious, but over time, it becomes second nature and offers a clear picture of your spending behavior.

Weekly budget check-ins are another powerful tool. They serve as a reflection point, a time to assess how closely your spending aligns with your budget. These check-ins are not about criticizing yourself for any deviation, but about understanding why they happen and how to address them. Were there unexpected expenses? Did you overspend on dining out? Use these sessions to adjust your budget if necessary, ensuring it remains realistic and effective. This regular review helps in catching small issues before they snowball into larger problems, keeping you on track toward your financial goals.

To effectively track your expenses, use tools that fit your lifestyle. Expense tracking spreadsheets are a great starting point. They offer a customizable way to log expenses, allowing you to categorize and analyze your spending. Automated expense reports, often available through budgeting apps, take this a step further. These reports can automatically categorize transactions, offering insights without manual entry. They save time and reduce errors, providing a comprehensive view of your financial health. Choose the tool that you find easiest to use consistently, as the best tool is the one you'll use regularly.

Analyzing your spending data is where the real magic happens. This analysis involves identifying spending patterns—those recurring expenses or impulse buys that quietly drain your finances. Once you spot these patterns, you can make informed adjustments. Calculate variances between your actual spending and your budgeted amounts. Are you consistently overspending in one category? This variance analysis helps pinpoint areas needing adjustment, guiding you to reallocate funds more effectively. Understanding this data empowers you to make proactive financial decisions rather than reactive ones, leading to better budget adherence and increased savings.

Accountability is a key factor in maintaining financial discipline. Consider joining budgeting communities, either online or in person. These communities provide support and share experiences, making budgeting a collective effort rather than a solitary task. They offer encouragement, share tips, and celebrate successes together. Another option is to find a financial mentor—someone with experience in managing money who can offer guidance and accountability. A mentor provides a personal touch, offering advice tailored to your unique financial situation. This relationship can inspire new ideas and foster a deeper understanding of financial management.

Reflection: Your Spending Story

Take a moment to reflect on your spending habits over the past month. What patterns do you notice? Are there categories where you consistently overspend? Write down your observations. This exercise is about awareness, not judgment. By understanding your habits, you can start to adjust them, aligning your spending with your financial goals. This reflection isn't just a one-time activity; make it a regular part of your financial routine. As you track and review your spending, you'll find it easier to stay accountable and make choices that support your long-term financial health.

ADJUSTING YOUR BUDGET FOR UNEXPECTED CHANGES

Life has a way of throwing curveballs when we least expect them. One day, you're comfortably managing your finances, and the next, an unforeseen event like a job loss or medical emergency disrupts everything. These moments are stark reminders of why flexibility in budgeting is crucial. A rigid budget may falter under unexpected pressure, but an adaptable one can absorb these shocks, allowing you to navigate life's unpredictability with confidence. Seasonal expenses, such as holidays, also demand flexibility. They can sneak up on you, leaving you unprepared if you haven't adjusted your financial plan to accommodate them. The goal is to build a budget that bends but doesn't break. This adaptability isn't just about surviving financial storms; it's about maintaining your progress toward financial goals, regardless of life's twists and turns.

One effective strategy for adjusting your budget in the face of unexpected changes is to re-evaluate discretionary spending. These are the areas where you have the most control, such as entertainment or dining out. By temporarily cutting back on these non-essential expenses, you can redirect funds to cover pressing needs or replenish your savings. Another strategy involves utilizing your emergency funds, which serve as a financial safety net during times of crisis. If you've been diligently saving for emergencies, now is the time to tap into those resources. Doing so can provide the financial cushion needed to weather the storm while keeping your long-term goals intact. It's important to remember that these funds should be replenished once you're back on stable ground, ensuring your prepared for any future surprises.

For those with irregular income sources, such as freelancers or seasonal workers, budgeting requires an additional layer of planning. Unlike a steady salary, freelance income can fluctuate dramatically from month to month. To manage this uncertainty, consider setting a baseline budget based on your lowest expected income. This conservative approach ensures that your essential needs are met, even during lean months. Any additional income can then be allocated toward savings or discretionary spending. Seasonal workers face similar challenges, with income spikes during busy periods and lulls in the off-season. Planning for these fluctuations involves saving a portion of your income during high-earning months to cover expenses during slower times. This proactive approach can prevent financial stress and help maintain a stable budget year-round.

Building a budget buffer is another key component of financial resilience. This buffer acts as a financial shock absorber, allowing you to manage unforeseen expenses without derailing your budget. To create a buffer, consider allocating a small portion of your monthly income to a separate savings account specifically for this purpose. Over time, even modest contributions can grow into a significant safety net. An emergency savings account is another effective tool for managing unexpected costs. By setting aside funds specifically for emergencies, you can address sudden expenses without dipping into your regular budget. This approach protects your financial stability and provides peace of mind, knowing you're prepared for whatever life throws your way.

In the context of adjusting your budget, flexibility is not just a strategy; it's a mindset. By embracing adaptability, you're better equipped to handle life's uncertainties while maintaining control of your financial trajectory. Remember, the goal isn't perfect but progress. A flexible budget allows you to remain focused on your long-term financial aspirations, even as you navigate the inevitable ups and downs of life. Through careful planning and a willingness to adjust, you can create a financial plan that supports you through every season of life.

OVERCOMING BUDGETING OBSTACLES: STAYING ON TRACK

The path to financial stability is often littered with challenges that can derail even the most well-intentioned budget. Emotional spending, for instance, is a common pitfall. It's that irrational urge to buy something unnecessary during times of stress or boredom, a temporary balm for deeper emotions. Recognizing these impulses is the first step. Ask yourself if the purchase truly aligns with your goals or if it's a quick fix to an emotional need. Developing strategies to redirect these urges into healthier activities, like exercising or engaging in hobbies, can be incredibly effective. Similarly, a lack of motivation can sneak in, making it difficult to stick to financial plans. To combat this, remind yourself of the bigger picture. Revisit your goals and visualize the freedom that comes with financial control. Sometimes, all it takes is a small reminder of your long-term aspirations to reignite your drive.

Cultivating a resilient mindset is paramount. Embrace budgeting as a tool of empowerment rather than a list of limitations. Positive financial affirmations can be remarkably powerful. Start each day with a mantra that reinforces your commitment and capability, such as "I control my financial destiny" or "Every small step brings me closer to my goals." These affirmations work to reshape your mindset, turning budgeting from a chore into an act of self-empowerment. Another technique is goal visualization. Take a moment to picture the life you want to achieve, the goals you are striving for, and how budgeting will help you get there. Visualization creates a mental image of success, serving as a constant motivation to stay the course.

Periodically reassessing your budgeting techniques ensures they remain effective and relevant to your evolving lifestyle. Conducting budget audits involves reviewing every aspect of your financial plan to identify what's working and what isn't. Are there areas where you consistently overspend? Is your income allocation still aligned with your goals? This introspection allows you to make informed adjustments, ensuring your budget continues to serve its purpose. Experimenting with new techniques can also breathe new life into your financial management. Perhaps a new app has emerged that better suits your needs, or maybe a different method of categorizing expenses could offer clearer insights. Be open to change and willing to adapt.

Recognizing and celebrating milestones is crucial to maintaining motivation throughout the budgeting process. Set small, achievable goals, and when you reach them, take the time to celebrate. This could be as simple as enjoying a modest treat or sharing your success with a friend. Implementing a reward system can reinforce positive financial behavior, making the journey to larger goals feel more attainable. Keeping track of these milestones in a dedicated journal or digital tracker can provide a visual representation of your progress, serving as a powerful motivator. As you see your successes accumulate, the broader vision of financial security becomes increasingly tangible.

In overcoming budgeting obstacles, remember that the journey is uniquely yours. Each step, whether forward or backward, offers a lesson. Embrace the learning process, adapt to changes, and maintain your focus on the desired outcome. The road may be long, but with persistence and resilience, financial freedom is within reach. As you continue to refine your budgeting practices, you'll find that the obstacles that once seemed insurmountable become mere stepping stones on your path to financial success.

CHAPTER 2
BUILDING AND UNDERSTANDING CREDIT

I remember the first time I checked my credit score. It was like peeking into a secret part of my financial life, revealing a number that held significant power over my future. This three-digit score, often shrouded in mystery, dictates so much: the interest rates on loans, the approval for rental applications, even the insurance premiums you might face. Yet, despite its importance, many young adults find themselves mystified by the intricacies of credit scores. Understanding these numbers isn't just beneficial—it's crucial for navigating the financial world with confidence.

Your credit score is a distillation of several factors, each contributing to your overall creditworthiness. At its core, the credit score breaks down into five primary components, each with its own weight. First and foremost is your payment history, making up 35% of your score. This aspect reflects your record of paying bills on time and is the most significant factor lenders consider (SOURCE 1). Next is credit utilization, accounting for 30%. It measures how much credit you're using compared to how much is available, indicating how reliant you are on borrowed money. The length of your credit history follows, contributing 15%. It assesses the age of your accounts, with older histories generally viewed more favorably. Finally, new credit and credit mix each make up 10%. New credit examines recent inquiries and accounts, while credit mix looks at the variety of credit types you manage, such as credit cards, loans, and other financial obligations.

Interpreting what these scores mean is the next step. Scores typically range from 300 to 850, with higher scores signaling to lenders that you're a lower risk. A score above 800 is often considered excellent and can open doors to the best interest rates and loan terms. A score between 740 and 799 is excellent, while 670 to 739 is generally viewed as good. Scores below this range may still allow for loan approval but often come with higher interest rates and less favorable terms. Understanding where you stand can help you assess your financial health and set realistic goals for improvement. This understanding is not just academic; it directly influences your ability to secure loans, rent an apartment, or even get a new cellphone plan.

The impact of your credit score extends beyond just borrowing. It influences various aspects of your financial life, often in subtle yet significant ways. For instance, the interest rate on a loan or credit card can vary dramatically depending on your score, with higher scores typically qualifying for lower rates. This can save you substantial amounts over the life of a loan. Credit scores also affect security deposits on utilities or rental agreements. A higher score might mean you pay less upfront when setting up services or renting a home. These nuances highlight why understanding and improving your credit score can have a profound effect on your overall financial picture.

Monitoring your credit score regularly is an essential practice. It helps you catch discrepancies early, protecting you from errors or fraudulent activity that could damage your score. There are several free resources available, such as annualcreditreport.com, where you can check your credit report from each of the three major credit bureaus—Experian, Equifax, and TransUnion—once a year. Consider staggering these checks throughout the year to maintain regular oversight. Monitoring your credit score is not just about keeping tabs; it's about staying informed and proactive in managing your financial health.

Reflection: Your Credit Score Health Check

Take a moment to reflect on your current credit score. If you haven't checked it recently, use one of the free resources mentioned to get an update. What does your score say about your financial health? Are there areas you can improve? Jot down your observations and any goals you might set to enhance your creditworthiness. This exercise will not only give you a clearer picture of where you stand, but also help you identify actionable steps toward a healthier financial future. Remember, your credit score is not just a number; it's a tool that, when understood and managed well, can lead to greater financial opportunities.

BUILDING CREDIT FROM SCRATCH: ESSENTIAL TIPS

Building credit from the ground up can feel like a daunting task, but it's a crucial step toward financial independence. Establishing initial credit lines when you have no prior history is a practical starting point. Consider secured credit cards, which are specifically designed for individuals new to credit. These cards require a cash deposit that serves as your credit limit. While it might seem limiting, it is a safe way to demonstrate responsible credit use. Over time, consistent use and timely payments can lead to eligibility for traditional credit cards. Another option is credit-builder loans offered by some banks and credit unions. These loans work by holding the borrowed amount in a savings account while you make payments. Once paid off, the funds are released to you, boosting your credit score in the process.

Another effective strategy is to become an authorized user on a responsible account, such as a family member's credit card. This method allows you to benefit from their established credit history, reflecting positively on your score. It's important to choose someone who pays their bills on time and maintains low balances. By piggybacking on their good habits, you're essentially laying a solid foundation for your credit profile. The shared credit history can significantly improve your credit score, providing a springboard for future credit opportunities. This strategy is especially beneficial for young adults who may not yet qualify for a credit card on their own.

One of the cornerstones of building credit is making consistent bill payments. This might sound straightforward, but it's vital to grasp the weight of this practice. On-time payments reflect positively on your credit report and signal to lenders that you're reliable. Consider setting up automatic payment setups to ensure you're never late. A missed payment can linger on your credit report for seven years, causing significant damage to your score and making future borrowing more expensive. The peace of mind that comes with knowing your bills are paid automatically is worth the few minutes it takes to set up. Plus, it saves you from the stress and potential fees associated with late payments.

Diversifying your credit types is another strategy to strengthen your credit profile. This involves having a mix of revolving credit, such as credit cards, and installment credit, like student loans or a car loan. Each type of credit demonstrates different aspects of financial management. For instance, revolving credit shows your ability to handle fluctuating balances, while installment credit reflects your commitment to long-term financial obligations. Even small personal loans can contribute to this mix, showcasing your ability to manage different credit products. Having various credit types isn't just beneficial for your score; it prepares you for real-world financial scenarios where managing multiple obligations is the norm.

Understanding these strategies and implementing them effectively can set you on a path to strong credit health. It's not merely about building a score; it's about creating a financial identity that will serve you well throughout life. As you take these steps, remember that building credit is a marathon, not a sprint. Patience, consistency, and responsible management are your best allies in this endeavor. Over time, these practices will not only strengthen your credit profile, but also open doors to financial opportunities you might not have thought possible.

RESPONSIBLE CREDIT CARD USE: AVOIDING DEBT TRAPS

Choosing the right credit card is a pivotal decision that can influence your financial health significantly. With a myriad of options available, it's easy to feel overwhelmed. Start by aligning your choice with your financial goals and spending habits. If minimizing interest payments is your priority, consider a low-interest credit card. These cards can save you money over time, especially if you plan to carry a balance. On the other hand, reward and cashback options can be beneficial if you pay off your balance each month. These cards offer incentives like travel points or cashback on purchases, turning everyday spending into tangible rewards. Assess your lifestyle and spending patterns to determine which types of card complements your financial strategy. Remember, the best card for you is one that fits your current needs and helps you to achieve your financial goals without unnecessary complications.

Using credit responsibly is the cornerstone of maintaining a healthy financial profile. One of the key practices is keeping your credit utilization below 30%. Utilization refers to the portion of your credit limit that you use, and staying under this threshold signals to lenders that you're managing your credit well. Another crucial habit is paying your balances in full each month. Doing so avoids costly interest charges and reinforces positive credit behavior. It's tempting to make just the minimum payment, especially when budgets are tight, but this approach can lead to a cycle of increasing debt due to accumulating interest. By committing to pay off your full balance, you set a strong foundation for a healthy credit history and financial discipline. These practices don't just benefit your credit score; they cultivate a mindset of financial responsibility and foresight.

Recognizing the warning signs of debt accumulation is essential for preventing financial pitfalls. One of the earliest indicators is reliance on minimum payments. If you find yourself unable to pay more than the minimum, it's a signal that your expenses may be outpacing your income. Consistent balance increases are another red flag. If your credit card balance keeps creeping up, it's time to evaluate your spending habits. This might involve cutting back on discretionary purchases or finding ways to increase your income. Being aware of these signs allows you to take corrective action before the situation becomes unmanageable. It's about staying vigilant and proactive in managing your finances, ensuring that you maintain control over your credit situation. By addressing these issues early, you can avoid the stress and financial strain that often accompany high levels of debt.

Strategies for managing credit card debt involve a mix of discipline and tactical planning. Setting spending limits is a straightforward yet effective method. By deciding in advance how much you can afford to spend each month, you create a boundary that helps prevent impulse buying. This strategy curtails unnecessary expenses and ensures that your spending aligns with your budget. Balance transfer options can be another tool in your financial toolkit. If you're carrying a high-interest balance, transferring it to a card with a lower or zero introductory interest rate can reduce the total amount of interest you pay. However, it's crucial to understand the terms and fees associated with balance transfers, ensuring that the benefits outweigh any costs. These strategies require careful consideration and planning, but when executed well, they can help you regain control over your credit card debt and steer your financial life back on track.

UNDERSTANDING CREDIT REPORTS: KEEPING SCORE

When you think about credit, often the first thing that comes to mind is your credit score. However, your credit report is equally important and provides a more profound insight into your financial behavior. A credit report is a detailed record that highlights your credit history. It includes several sections, each playing a pivotal role in assessing your creditworthiness. The first section is personal information. This part contains basic details like your name, address, and social security number. It's crucial to keep this information up-to-date to avoid any confusion or mix-ups in your credit report. Next, you'll find credit account details. This section lists out your credit accounts, detailing the type of credit (like credit cards or loans), the account balance, and your payment history. It gives a comprehensive view of how you handle credit, reflecting your reliability and financial habits. This part of the report is particularly scrutinized by lenders when you apply for new credit.

Accessing your credit report is a right, not a privilege. In the United States, you can obtain a free credit report annually from each of the three major credit bureaus—Experian, Equifax, and TransUnion. Visit annualcreditreport.com, the only government-sanctioned site, to request these reports. It's wise to stagger these requests throughout the year to monitor your credit regularly. By doing so, you maintain a steady watch on your financial health. Besides the annual free reports, you can also request additional reports online, though these may come with a fee. Regular review of your credit report is essential; it helps you spot any discrepancies or errors that could impact your credit score. Remember, your credit report is a reflection of your financial responsibility and can influence your ability to secure loans, rent an apartment, or even get a job.

Errors on credit reports are more common than you might think, and they can have serious consequences if left unaddressed. Common errors include incorrect personal information, accounts that don't belong to you, and incorrect account statuses, such as showing a closed account as open. Spotting these inaccuracies early is crucial. If you find any discrepancies, take immediate action. The dispute process involves contacting both the credit reporting company and the company that provided the incorrect information (SOURCE 3). You'll need to provide a written explanation of the error, along with supporting documents. This dispute should be sent via certified mail to ensure it's received. Upon receiving your dispute, the credit reporting company must investigate and report back. If your dispute is successful, the error will be corrected, which could lead to an improved credit score.

Your credit report is not just a snapshot of your financial past; it's a tool you can use to enhance your credit health. Start by analyzing your debt-to-income ratio, which compares your monthly debt payments to your monthly income. A high ratio can be a red flag to lenders, indicating you might struggle to manage additional debt. Understanding this ratio can help you make adjustments to improve your financial standing. Next, look for areas where you can improve. Perhaps you notice a pattern of late payments. Setting up automatic payments or reminders might help. Or maybe you see that your credit utilization is high. Paying down existing debt could boost your score. By leveraging the insights from your credit report, you can make informed decisions to strengthen your financial future.

REPAIRING POOR CREDIT: STEPS TO RECOVERY

Facing the reality of poor credit can feel overwhelming, but the first step toward recovery is understanding the extent of the damage. Begin by scrutinizing your credit report in detail. Look for negative accounts, such as late payments, defaults, or collections, as these directly impact your score. Identifying these issues helps you prioritize which areas need immediate attention. Perhaps there's a credit card with a history of missed payments or a loan that was defaulted. By pinpointing these trouble spots, you set the stage for a targeted repair strategy. It's not just about knowing what went wrong; it's about devising a plan to make things right.

Once you've assessed the damage, it's time to create a structured credit repair plan. Start by setting realistic credit goals. Maybe you aim to increase your credit score by 50 points over the next year or to pay off a specific debt. Clear goals provide direction and motivation. Next, develop a payment plan that aligns with these goals. This might involve setting aside a certain amount each month to tackle outstanding debts. Consider using tools like budgeting apps to track your progress and ensure you're staying on course. A well-thought-out plan helps in managing your current debts and lays the foundation for healthier financial habits in the future.

Negotiating with creditors is a powerful tool in credit repair. Many creditors are willing to negotiate terms if it means they'll eventually recover what's owed. Start by reaching out with a goodwill letter, especially if you have a history of good payments that was disrupted by a temporary hardship. Explain your situation honestly and ask if they might remove a negative mark as a gesture of goodwill. In some cases, creditors might agree to modify your payment plan, offering more manageable terms or even settlements. These negotiations can lead to the removal of negative items from your report, significantly improving your credit score. Remember, it never hurts to ask, and the potential benefits can be substantial.

Monitoring your progress is crucial throughout this recovery process. Regularly check your credit score to track changes and celebrate milestones, no matter how small. Did your score increase by five points? That's progress worth acknowledging. Keeping track of these improvements reinforces the positive changes you're making and keeps you motivated to continue. Set reminders to review your credit report periodically, ensuring that errors are corrected and that your efforts are reflected in your score. This consistent monitoring helps you stay committed to your credit repair plan and provides the encouragement needed to persevere through the ups and downs of rebuilding your credit.

CREDIT MYTHS DEBUNKED: SEPARATING FACT FROM FICTION

In the world of credit, myths abound, often leading people astray. One common misconception is that closing unused credit accounts can boost your credit score. Many believe that by shutting down these dormant lines, they're streamlining their credit profile. In reality, closing accounts can actually harm your score. This is because it reduces your total available credit, thus increasing your credit utilization ratio. A higher utilization ratio suggests to lenders that you might be over-reliant on credit, which can negatively impact your score. Keeping unused accounts open, provided they don't carry annual fees, can help maintain a healthy credit utilization rate.

Another widespread myth is that checking your own credit score will damage it. This belief likely stems from confusion between hard and soft inquiries. A hard inquiry occurs when a lender checks your credit as part of a loan application, which can slightly lower your score. However, checking your own credit is considered a soft inquiry and doesn't affect your score at all. Regularly monitoring your credit score is a savvy financial move, allowing you to catch errors and track your progress without repercussions. This myth, if believed, can prevent you from taking an active role in managing your financial health.

Understanding the truth about building credit involves embracing diverse credit types. Many people assume having only one type of credit is sufficient. However, having a mix of credit types, such as credit cards and installment loans, can enhance your credit profile. This diversity shows lenders that you can manage different financial products responsibly. Additionally, there's a misconception about credit inquiries. While multiple inquiries in a short time can raise red flags, periodic checks, especially when shopping for loans, are often treated as a single inquiry. This practice can prevent unnecessary score drops and encourage you to seek the best rates.

These myths can lead to poor financial decisions. Misguided beliefs about credit card usage might prompt individuals to carry a balance, thinking it benefits their score. In truth, carrying a balance incurs interest and doesn't improve your credit score. Paying off balances in full each month is more beneficial. Similarly, the avoidance of credit checks, due to the mistaken belief that they harm scores, can result in missed opportunities to detect errors or fraud. This avoidance can leave you blind to potential problems on your credit report, impacting your financial stability over time.

It's crucial to educate yourself and others about these myths. Sharing accurate credit information within your community can empower others to make informed decisions. Hosting educational sessions at local community centers or schools can be an excellent way to spread knowledge. Use social media platforms to share articles or tips about credit management. By dispelling myths and promoting facts, you can help create a more financially literate community. This collective effort ensures that more people have access to the knowledge they need to manage their credit effectively.

As we wrap up this chapter, it's clear that understanding credit goes beyond just knowing your score. It's about being aware of the myths and facts that can shape your financial decisions. By debunking these myths, you equip yourself with the tools to build and maintain a healthy credit profile. This knowledge not only benefits you but also those around you, creating a ripple effect of financial empowerment. Next, we'll explore how to effectively manage and leverage savings and investments, building on the solid foundation of credit management.

CHAPTER 3
SAVING AND INVESTING FOR THE FUTURE

Imagine a sudden car breakdown on a busy highway or an unexpected medical bill arriving just when you thought you had your finances in order. These scenarios can quickly derail financial stability, but having an emergency fund serves as a protective cushion against such unforeseen events. An emergency fund is like a financial safety net, offering peace of mind and security when life's unpredictable moments strike. It's not just about having money set aside; it's about creating a buffer that shields you from the stress of relying on high-interest credit cards or loans, which can lead to a debt spiral that's difficult to escape. Emergencies can range from sudden car repairs and urgent medical expenses to temporary loss of income, each requiring immediate attention and funds ready at hand.

Determining the appropriate size for your emergency fund is crucial and should align with your personal circumstances. A common guideline is to save enough to cover 3–6 months' worth of living expenses. This range offers a balance between being prepared for longer-term crises and not tying up too much cash that could be used for other financial goals. Consider factors like job stability and health when setting your target. If you work in a volatile industry, you might aim for the higher end of the range. Conversely, if your employment is stable, a three-month cushion might suffice. Personal health considerations are also key; if you have ongoing medical needs, a larger fund could prevent financial strain from unexpected health-related costs.

Building an emergency fund might seem daunting, but with the right strategies, it becomes manageable. Start by automating your savings. Set up automatic transfers from your checking account to a designated savings account every payday. This method ensures that you consistently contribute to your fund without the temptation to spend the money elsewhere. Another effective approach is to capitalize on windfalls and tax refunds. Whenever you receive extra money, such as a bonus from work or a tax return, allocate a portion of it to your emergency fund. These occasional boosts can significantly accelerate your savings progress, helping you reach your target faster.

Once you've established your fund, maintaining and replenishing it is equally important. Treat your emergency savings as a non-negotiable expense, much like paying rent or utilities. This mindset helps prioritize it in your financial planning. Periodically review your fund to ensure it remains aligned with your current needs and expenses. If you've had to dip into it, plan to rebuild it as soon as possible. Regular reviews also allow you to adjust your savings target if your circumstances change, such as a salary increase or a shift in your living situation. Remember, your emergency fund is not just a pool of money; it's an investment in your future peace of mind.

Reflection: Your Emergency Fund Plan

Consider where you currently stand with your emergency savings. Do you have a dedicated fund? If so, how much is in it, and does it align with your current financial situation and risks? If not, what steps can you take to start building one? Jot down your thoughts and create a simple action plan. This reflection is about understanding your preparedness and taking actionable steps toward financial security. Regularly revisiting this plan can help ensure you're always ready for whatever life throws your way.

SAVING STRATEGIES FOR BIG GOALS: PLANNING AHEAD

Identifying your big financial goals is like setting the stage for your future. Whether you're dreaming of owning a car, funding further education, or perhaps planning for a major life event, these aspirations need clarity and prioritization. Short-term goals, such as saving for a new gadget or a weekend getaway, differ vastly from long-term ambitions like buying a home or retiring comfortably. Start by listing your goals, categorizing them into short-term and long-term, and then rank them by importance. This process doesn't just organize your thoughts; it creates a roadmap that guides your saving efforts. It's about understanding what you truly want to achieve and laying the groundwork to make those dreams a reality.

Once your goals are clear, it's time to create a structured savings plan. This isn't a one-size-fits-all scenario; your plan should reflect your unique financial situation and goals. Begin by calculating how much you need to contribute each month to reach your savings milestones. Use goal-specific savings accounts to keep your funds organized and earmarked for their intended purpose. These accounts can also help you resist the temptation to dip into your savings for everyday expenses. By automating your savings contributions, you ensure consistency and avoid relying on willpower alone. Regular deposits, even if small, build up over time, bringing you steadily closer to your goals. Remember, the key is not just to save, but to save with intention and strategy, aligning your actions with your aspirations.

Tracking your progress is crucial to staying on course. Regular check-ins on your savings balance provide insight into how well you're sticking to your plan. Set aside time each month to review your progress, celebrating how far you've come and identifying areas for improvement. If you find yourself falling short, consider adjusting your contributions. Perhaps unexpected expenses have cropped up, or your income has changed. Flexibility is essential; your savings plan should adapt to your life, not the other way around. By remaining vigilant and open to adjustments, you maintain momentum toward achieving your financial goals. This process isn't static; it evolves with you, reflecting changes in your life and priorities.

Motivation plays a significant role in maintaining a savings habit. One effective technique is to use visual goal tracking charts. These charts provide a tangible representation of your progress, making the abstract concept of saving more concrete. Each update brings a sense of accomplishment, motivating you to keep going. Additionally, set small rewards for reaching milestones along the way. These incentives don't have to be extravagant; a simple treat or a day off can reinforce your commitment and make the journey enjoyable. By turning savings into a rewarding experience, you reach your goals and cultivate a positive relationship with money. It's about creating a system that supports you, celebrating the small victories as you work towards the larger ones.

INVESTING 101: GETTING STARTED WITH LIMITED FUNDS

Dipping your toes into the world of investing can feel intimidating, especially when complex jargon like stocks, bonds, and mutual funds starts flying around. Let's break these down into digestible concepts. Stocks represent ownership in a company, offering you a slice of the pie and, potentially, a share in the profits. Bonds, on the other hand, are essentially loans you give to a corporation or government, promising regular interest payments over time. Mutual funds pool money from multiple investors to purchase a diversified portfolio of stocks and bonds, managed by financial professionals. Understanding these basic terms is your first step into investing, demystifying what can seem an opaque world. At the heart of investing lies the dynamic between risk and reward. Higher potential returns typically involve more risk, while safer investments often yield lower returns. Knowing this balance is key to making informed decisions.

Starting small is the path for many young investors, especially when funds are limited. Micro-investment platforms like Acorns offer a gentle entry into investing by rounding up your everyday purchases to the nearest dollar and investing the difference. This method makes investing feel less daunting, as it allows you to grow your portfolio incrementally without feeling the pinch in your wallet. Another option to consider is fractional shares, where you can buy a portion of a stock rather than a whole share. This approach provides you with access to high-priced stocks that might otherwise be unreachable, enabling diversification even on a budget. Both strategies allow you to build investment habits early, setting the stage for future growth.

When it comes to investing, setting clear goals is as important as the investments themselves. Your choices should reflect your personal financial objectives, whether they're short-term needs like buying a car or long-term dreams such as funding retirement. Align your investment horizon with your goals; short-term goals might benefit from less volatile investments, while long-term goals can afford more risk for potentially higher returns. Balancing growth and safety is crucial. Younger investors often lean towards growth, given the time they have to weather market fluctuations. However, maintaining a mix of safe assets can provide a buffer against volatility, ensuring that your portfolio can withstand both the highs and the lows of the market.

Arming yourself with knowledge is fundamental to becoming a confident investor. Fortunately, there are numerous resources available to expand your understanding of the financial markets. Books remain a timeless resource, offering in-depth insights into investing principles and strategies. Podcasts are another engaging medium, delivering expert discussions and tips directly to your ears while you commute or exercise. Online courses can guide you through the complexities of finance at your own pace, offering structured learning tailored to your level of experience. Investment apps, many of which come with built-in educational tools, can also serve as both a platform for managing your investments and a resource for learning. These tools are invaluable for beginners, providing the foundation needed to make informed investment choices. They empower you to navigate the financial landscape with confidence, transforming what might initially seem a daunting task into an exciting opportunity for growth.

As you embark on your investing adventure, remember that knowledge is power. The more you learn and engage with these resources, the more equipped you'll be to make decisions that align with your financial goals and risk tolerance. Investing isn't just about making money; it's about building a future that reflects your ambitions and secures your financial well-being. With the right tools and a willingness to learn, you'll find that investing is not only accessible but also an empowering part of your financial journey.

UNDERSTANDING RISK: FINDING YOUR COMFORT ZONE

Navigating the world of investments inevitably involves understanding various types of risks that can impact your returns. Market risk, for instance, is the possibility of experiencing losses due to factors that affect the overall performance of the financial markets. It's the roller-coaster ride of stock prices driven by economic changes, political events, or natural disasters. Then there's credit risk, which comes into play when a borrower might fail to meet their obligations, causing the lender to lose money. This is especially relevant if you're considering bonds, where the issuer's ability to repay can significantly alter your returns. Liquidity risk is another factor to consider. It refers to the ease with which you can buy or sell an asset without affecting its price. Assets that are not easily traded might require you to sell discounted, impacting your overall investment strategy. These risks contribute to the volatility of your portfolio, the wild swings that can make even seasoned investors uneasy. Understanding these concepts is key to making informed decisions that align with your financial goals.

Before diving into investments, it's important to assess your personal risk tolerance. This involves gauging how much risk you're comfortable taking on, which can be influenced by your financial situation, investment goals, and even your personality. Risk tolerance is not a one-size-fits-all scenario; it varies from person to person. One effective way to evaluate this is through risk assessment questionnaires, which can provide insights into your comfort level with potential losses. These assessments often ask about your reaction to market downturns or financial setbacks, helping you understand your emotional responses to risk. Balancing emotional comfort with financial ambition is crucial. While everyone wants high returns, the stress of volatile investments might not be worth it if you lose sleep over market movements. Finding that sweet spot where financial strategy meets peace of mind is the goal.

Once you've identified your risk tolerance, it's time to consider strategies for mitigating investment risk. Diversification techniques are fundamental in this regard. By spreading your investments across different asset classes, you reduce the impact of a poor performance in any single area. Think of it as not putting all your eggs in one basket. Diversification allows you to balance potential losses with gains in other sectors, creating a more stable overall portfolio. Another strategy is setting stop-loss orders, which automatically sell an asset when its price falls to a certain level. This tactic helps limit potential losses without requiring you to monitor the market constantly. These strategies can be tailored to fit your personal risk profile, offering a buffer against unforeseen market events. By employing these techniques, you can create a robust portfolio that withstands turbulence.

Balancing risk and reward is the cornerstone of successful investing. It's about finding a balance that aligns with your individual financial goals and risk tolerance. Creating a risk-adjusted portfolio involves selecting investments that match your comfort level, ensuring that you're not taking on more risk than you're prepared to handle. Rebalancing your investments periodically is crucial to maintaining this balance. As market conditions shift, your portfolio's composition might stray from your original plan. Regularly reviewing and adjusting your investments can help realign them with your goals, optimizing potential returns while managing risk. This ongoing process is part of maintaining a dynamic investment strategy that evolves with changing conditions. Balancing risk and reward isn't about eliminating risk entirely—it's about managing it in a way that supports your financial objectives while providing a sense of security.

DIVERSIFYING YOUR INVESTMENTS: A BEGINNER'S GUIDE

Diversification is a fundamental principle in investing, often likened to not putting all your eggs in one basket. Its importance cannot be overstated, as it plays a vital role in managing risk and stabilizing returns. By spreading your investments across different asset classes, you reduce reliance on the performance of a single asset. Think about it this way: if one investment underperforms, others in diverse sectors or classes may perform well, balancing out potential losses. This strategy helps protect your portfolio from the volatility that can come with investing in just one type of asset. Diversification creates a buffer, allowing you to weather financial storms with greater ease, offering a more stable return over time. It's about creating a safety net that ensures your financial goals are not derailed by market fluctuations.

There are various strategies to diversify your portfolio effectively. Geographic diversification involves investing in markets across different countries or regions. This approach mitigates the risk associated with economic downturns in any single nation. For example, if the U.S. market faces a downturn, investments in Asia or Europe could continue to perform well, balancing your overall portfolio. Asset class diversification is another critical strategy. This involves spreading investments across different types of assets, such as stocks, bonds, and real estate. Each asset class reacts differently to market conditions, offering unique opportunities for growth and stability. Stocks may offer higher returns but come with more risk, while bonds typically provide steadier, albeit lower, returns. Real estate can offer a hedge against inflation and add tangible value to your investment mix. Embracing these diversification strategies can significantly enhance your portfolio's resilience.

Building a diversified portfolio requires thoughtful allocation across various sectors and industries. Start by evaluating different sectors, such as technology, healthcare, and consumer goods, to identify potential growth opportunities. Allocating investments across these sectors minimizes the impact of poor performance in a single industry. Index funds and ETFs

(Exchange-Traded Funds) are excellent tools for achieving diversification with ease. These investment vehicles pool money from numerous investors to buy a wide array of assets, providing instant diversification. They often track specific indices, such as the S&P 500, giving you exposure to a broad market segment. By investing in index funds or ETFs, you can benefit from diversification without needing to research and select individual stocks or bonds. This approach simplifies the diversification process and makes it accessible to investors at any experience level.

Once your diversified portfolio is established, monitoring and adjusting it regularly is crucial. Market conditions and personal financial goals can shift over time, necessitating portfolio adjustments. Regularly reviewing your investments helps ensure they remain aligned with your objectives. Responding to market changes might involve reallocating assets to capitalize on emerging opportunities or selling underperforming investments to minimize losses. It's also essential to align your portfolio with evolving financial goals. As your life circumstances change, such as approaching retirement or starting a family, your investment strategy should adapt accordingly. Rebalancing your portfolio periodically ensures it reflects your current risk tolerance and financial objectives, maintaining the balance between risk and reward. This ongoing evaluation and adjustment process is key to sustaining a healthy, diversified portfolio that supports long-term financial success.

THE POWER OF COMPOUND INTEREST: GROWING YOUR MONEY

Compound interest is often hailed as one of the most powerful forces in finance, and for good reason. At its core, compound interest is the process where the interest earned on an investment is reinvested, allowing you to earn interest on your initial principal as well as on the accumulated interest from previous periods. This phenomenon, where your money starts to generate its own money, can lead to exponential growth over time. Unlike simple interest, which is calculated only on the principal amount, compound interest grows your wealth by reinvesting earnings, effectively compounding your returns. This concept is not just a mathematical curiosity; it's a practical tool for wealth building. The longer your money is invested, the more powerful compounding becomes, turning modest savings into significant sums over decades.

Time is the critical factor that enhances the effects of compound interest. Starting early can make a world of difference in the outcomes of your investments. Consider two scenarios: one where you begin investing at 25 and another at 35. Even if both investors contribute the same amount monthly, the one who starts earlier will have a significantly larger nest egg by retirement. This disparity is due to the exponential growth curve that compound interest follows. The longer your money is working for you, the more opportunity it has to grow, creating a snowball effect. Each year builds upon the last, magnifying your returns in a way that seems almost magical.

This is why financial experts often stress the importance of starting to invest as soon as possible.

To maximize the benefits of compound interest, there are several strategies you can employ. Reinvesting dividends is a straightforward yet effective approach. Rather than taking dividends as cash payouts, reinvest them into additional shares of your investment. This reinvestment increases the amount of money earning interest, further enhancing the compounding effect. Additionally, consider increasing your investment contributions over time. As your income grows, raise the amount you invest. Even small increases can have a significant impact over the long term. This strategy not only leverages compound interest but also aligns your investing habits with your financial growth, creating a virtuous cycle of wealth accumulation.

However, to truly harness the power of compounding, it's crucial to avoid common pitfalls that can undermine its effectiveness. One major mistake is withdrawing investments prematurely. Early withdrawals can disrupt the compounding process, reducing the potential for long-term growth. It's important to maintain a long-term perspective, allowing your investments to mature and multiply. Another consideration is fees and taxes, which can erode your returns if not managed properly. Pay attention to the fees associated with investment accounts and seek tax-efficient investment strategies. By being mindful of these factors, you can ensure that compound interest works to your advantage, helping you build and preserve wealth over time.

The principles of compound interest extend far beyond mere numbers. They represent a mindset of patience and foresight, emphasizing the value of time in financial growth. By understanding and applying these principles, you lay the groundwork for a financially secure future, where your money does more than just sit idle—it actively contributes to your wealth. As we move forward, we'll explore more advanced financial strategies that build upon the foundation of saving and investing, equipping you with the knowledge to navigate the complexities of personal finance with confidence.

CHAPTER 4
EFFECTIVE DEBT MANAGEMENT

Picture this: you're fresh out of college, degree in hand, ready to conquer the world. But wait—there's a shadow looming over your newfound freedom. It's student loans, a reality for many young adults embarking on their careers. Understanding and managing these loans can feel like navigating a labyrinth. Yet, mastering this aspect of your financial life is crucial for your peace of mind and future prosperity. Student loans, often seen as a necessary burden, are a pivotal part of your financial landscape. They can open doors to education and opportunities, but also weigh heavily if mismanaged. Let's embark on a journey to demystify student loans, ensuring they remain a stepping stone rather than a stumbling block.

Understanding the types of student loans is your first step. Federal student loans, such as Direct Loans, usually offer more favorable terms. They come with fixed interest rates and offer various repayment plans designed to accommodate different financial situations. One notable advantage of federal loans is the potential for income-driven repayment plans, which adjust your monthly payments based on your income and family size. This flexibility can ease the financial strain during times of low-income or career transitions. On the other hand, private student loans often come with variable interest rates and less flexible terms. These loans are typically based on your creditworthiness and may require a co-signer, making them riskier if your financial situation changes unexpectedly. Understanding these differences helps you make informed decisions about managing your debt effectively.

Exploring repayment plans is crucial in managing your student loans. The standard repayment plan is the default option, requiring fixed monthly payments over ten years. While this plan can save you money in interest, the payments may be higher than other options. Income-driven repayment plans, such as the SAVE plan, offer an alternative for those who need lower monthly payments. These plans base your payments on your income, offering relief during financially challenging times. They can also extend the repayment period, reducing the immediate burden but potentially increasing the total interest paid over time. Carefully evaluating your financial situation and future earning potential is key to choosing the right repayment plan for you. Consider your current income, job stability, and long-term financial goals when making this decision.

Making extra payments can significantly reduce the burden of student loans. By applying additional funds to your principal balance, you can reduce the interest accrued over the life of the loan. One effective strategy is the bi-weekly payment method. Instead of making one monthly payment, divide it in half and pay that amount every two weeks. This approach results in an extra month's payment each year, helping you pay off the loan faster and saving on interest. Another approach is to apply any windfalls, such as tax refunds or bonuses, directly to your loan principal. This tactic reduces the principal amount, leading to lower interest costs and a shorter repayment period. These strategies alleviate the financial burden and empower you to take control of your debt.

For those seeking additional relief, forgiveness programs can be a viable option. Public Service Loan Forgiveness (PSLF) offers forgiveness for federal loans after ten years of qualifying payments while working for a government or non-profit organization. This program can be a game-changer for those dedicated to public service careers. Teacher Loan Forgiveness is another option, providing up to $17,500 in forgiveness for teachers who serve in low-income schools for five consecutive years. These programs have specific eligibility requirements and application processes, so it's essential to research and ensure you meet the criteria. Understanding and pursuing these opportunities can significantly reduce your student loan burden, allowing you to focus on building your career and achieving financial stability.

Exercise: Your Student Loan Strategy

Take a moment to assess your student loan situation. List

the types of loans you have and the current repayment plans. Consider your income and employment status. Are there opportunities to make extra payments or explore forgiveness programs? Write down your observations and any action steps you plan to take. This exercise will help you gain clarity and confidence in managing your student loans effectively.

UNDERSTANDING INTEREST RATES: HOW THEY IMPACT DEBT

The world of interest rates can seem complex, but understanding them is key to managing debt effectively. Interest rates come in two main types: fixed and variable. Fixed interest rates remain constant throughout the life of a loan, providing predictability in monthly payments. This stability is particularly reassuring if you're budgeting carefully, as you know exactly what to expect each month, regardless of market fluctuations. On the other hand, variable interest rates fluctuate over time, usually in response to changes in the broader economic environment. These rates might start lower than fixed rates, offering immediate savings, but they carry the risk of increasing, which can lead to higher payments down the line. Understanding these differences allows you to choose the loan type that best fits your financial situation and risk tolerance.

Calculating the total interest cost over the life of a loan helps you grasp the long-term impact of your borrowing decisions. This involves creating an amortization schedule, which outlines each payment's division between principal and interest.

At the beginning of a loan, a larger portion of your payment goes toward interest, with the principal balance decreasing slowly. Over time, this balance shifts, and more of each payment reduces the principal. By examining an amortization schedule, you can see how much interest you'll pay over the loan's term. This knowledge can be eye-opening, highlighting the true cost of borrowing beyond just the monthly payments. Understanding the balance between interest and principal is crucial for making informed financial decisions and planning your debt repayment strategy.

There are several strategies you can employ to minimize the interest paid on your loans. Refinancing is one option, which involves replacing your current loan with a new one at a lower interest rate. This can reduce your monthly payments and the total interest paid over the life of the loan. However, it's important to consider any fees and the impact on your loan term before proceeding. Another effective strategy is paying more than the minimum required each month. By directing extra funds toward the principal, you reduce the amount of interest that accrues, effectively shortening the loan term and saving money. Consistently making additional payments, even small ones, can significantly lower the overall cost of your debt.

Interest rates also play a critical role in shaping your credit score and borrowing power. A lower interest rate suggests to lenders that you are a lower-risk borrower, positively influencing your credit score. Conversely, high-interest rates can indicate financial strain, potentially reducing your creditworthiness. Maintaining a good credit score helps secure favorable interest rates and impacts long-term financial health. Lower rates mean less money spent on interest, freeing up funds for savings and investments. This can enhance your financial stability and provide more opportunities to achieve your financial goals. Understanding the interplay between interest rates and credit can empower you to make more strategic financial decisions, ensuring you're leveraging your borrowing power effectively.

PRIORITIZING DEBT PAYMENTS: SNOWBALL VS. AVALANCHE

When facing a mountain of debt, it can feel like you're trying to climb a steep hill with no end in sight. But with the right strategy, reaching the summit is possible. One popular method is the debt snowball approach, which focuses on paying off the smallest debts first. Think of it as gaining momentum with each quick win. By eliminating smaller debts, you create a series of small victories that boost your morale and confidence. This psychological benefit can be incredibly motivating, especially if you're someone who feels overwhelmed by the thought of tackling larger financial obligations. As each small debt disappears, you gain a sense of accomplishment, encouraging you to keep going. It's like watching your progress unfold in real-time, giving you the push needed to tackle bigger challenges.

On the other hand, the debt avalanche method takes a more analytical approach by targeting debts with the highest interest rates first. By prioritizing these debts, you minimize the overall interest paid over time, leading to significant long-term savings. This method requires discipline and a strategic mindset, as it may take longer to see the results compared to the snowball method. However, the financial benefits are undeniable. By focusing on high-interest debts, you reduce the total amount you owe more efficiently, freeing up funds for other financial goals. This approach is particularly appealing to those who are driven by numbers and are willing to wait a bit longer for the tangible payoff. It's a method that requires patience but rewards you with substantial savings eventually.

Choosing the right method depends on your personal financial situation and emotional preferences. Conducting a personal financial assessment is a good starting point. Consider your income, expenses, and the types of debt you carry. Are you someone who thrives on quick wins, or do you prefer a method that maximizes savings? Emotional considerations are equally important. If you find motivation waning easily, the snowball method might be your best bet. Alternatively, if you're more concerned about the financial impact, the avalanche approach could be a better fit. There's no one-size-fits-all solution, so it's crucial to choose a strategy that aligns with your financial goals and mindset.

For those who can't decide between the two, a hybrid approach offers a personalized solution. By combining elements of both methods, you can tailor a plan that suits your unique needs. Start by paying off a few small debts to build momentum, then switch to targeting high-interest obligations. This flexibility allows you to adapt to changing circumstances, ensuring your plan remains effective over time. Tailoring payment plans in this way provides the best of both worlds, giving you the psychological boost of early victories while also addressing the financial benefits of reduced interest. Flexibility in switching methods ensures that you remain in control of your debt repayment journey, adapting as needed to stay on track.

CONSOLIDATION AND REFINANCING: ARE THEY RIGHT FOR YOU?

Debt consolidation often appears as a beacon of hope for those juggling multiple debts. Imagine the relief of replacing several payments with one single monthly obligation. This is the allure of debt consolidation: simplicity. By combining various debts into one, you manage a single payment, which can significantly reduce the chaos of handling several due dates and interest rates. Often, consolidation can also lower your interest rates, which means more of your payment goes to reducing the principal balance rather than just covering accrued interest. However, it's not a one-size-fits-all solution. The benefits of consolidation must be weighed against potential drawbacks, such as fees and the impact on your credit score, which may initially dip due to the new credit inquiry and account opening. Yet, for many, the streamlined process and potential savings can make it an attractive option.

Refinancing offers another path to potentially lower your debt burden, especially if you've seen an improvement in your credit score or if market interest rates have dropped since you first took out your loan. This process involves replacing an existing loan with a new one, ideally at a lower interest rate. Refinancing can be particularly advantageous for student loans and mortgages. For student loans, this might mean shifting from a federal plan to a private lender with a lower rate, though this often involves losing federal protections like income-driven repayment options. Mortgage refinancing, on the other hand, can significantly reduce monthly payments or the total amount of interest paid over the loan's life, especially when rates fall considerably. However, it's crucial to consider the costs associated with refinancing, such as closing fees, and weigh them against the potential savings.

Eligibility for consolidation and refinancing largely hinges on your credit score, as lenders look for evidence that you can manage your debts responsibly. A higher score can unlock better terms, allowing you to reap the full benefits of these financial tools. However, it's not just about the score; lenders will also assess your income stability and existing debt load. Risks include extending the life of your debt, which might lower monthly payments but increase the total cost over time. This is why evaluating the impact on your loan terms and total cost is essential. A consolidation or refinancing plan might offer immediate relief but could result in more paid interest eventually. Understanding these trade-offs is key to making an informed decision that aligns with your financial goals.

When considering consolidation or refinancing, conducting a thorough cost-benefit analysis helps illuminate the potential advantages and disadvantages. Start by calculating the total cost of your current debt situation, including remaining principal and interest. Then, compare it to the projected cost after consolidation or refinancing. Factor in any fees associated with the process, as these can eat into your savings. If the analysis shows significant savings and aligns with your long-term financial goals, these options might be beneficial. However, if the costs outweigh the benefits, or if the new terms extend your debt well into the future, it might be better to explore other avenues for debt reduction. Remember, the ultimate goal is to create a sustainable financial plan that supports your ambitions, providing clarity and stability as you move forward.

AVOIDING COMMON DEBT TRAPS: STAYING DEBT-FREE

Debt can feel like quicksand, pulling you deeper with every misstep. One of the most treacherous traps is predatory lending. These schemes often appear as lifelines, offering immediate cash without the scrutiny of a credit check. Payday loans are a notorious example. They promise fast relief but come with sky-high interest rates and fees that can quickly spiral out of control if not repaid immediately. Similarly, high-interest personal loans might seem like a viable option for quick cash, but they often come with hidden fees and exorbitant rates that can double or triple the initial amount borrowed. Identifying these predatory practices is crucial. Look for lenders who promise too-good-to-be-true offers and always read the fine print. A legitimate lender will outline all terms clearly and will not pressure you into immediate decisions. By being vigilant, you can avoid these traps and keep your financial health intact.

Another insidious trap is the cycle of revolving credit. Credit cards, when used wisely, can be a powerful tool. Yet, they can also lead to a cycle of debt that feels impossible to escape. The allure of making only minimum payments is tempting, especially when budgets are tight. However, this strategy barely covers interest and allows the principal to linger, leading to negative amortization. Over time, you end up paying much more than the original amount borrowed. This cycle is compounded by the revolving nature of credit cards, which allows you to continue borrowing even as your balance grows. Breaking free requires discipline and a strategic approach. Start by setting clear spending limits and sticking to them. This helps ensure that you only spend what you can afford to pay off at the end of the month, preventing the accumulation of debt.

Building healthy credit habits is essential for long-term financial stability. One effective strategy is to set spending limits that align with your budget. This practice prevents over-spending and helps you stay within the safe zone of credit utilization, ideally below 30%. Regular debt assessments are another important habit. Periodically reviewing your credit report allows you to monitor your progress and identify areas that need improvement. This proactive approach helps catch potential issues before they become significant problems. It also gives you an opportunity to celebrate your successes, reinforcing positive behaviors. By maintaining these habits, you lay the groundwork for a solid financial future, free from the stress of overwhelming debt.

When faced with complex debt situations, seeking professional advice can provide clarity and guidance. Credit counseling services offer support and education, helping you understand your financial situation and develop a plan to address it. These services often provide personalized advice tailored to your unique circumstances, offering insights that might be difficult to see from within your financial bubble. Financial planning professionals can also be invaluable allies, offering strategies to manage debt effectively while building wealth for the future. They bring a wealth of knowledge and experience, helping you navigate the complexities of debt repayment and financial planning. Consulting with these experts can provide a fresh perspective and empower you to take control of your financial destiny.

DEALING WITH DEBT COLLECTORS: KNOW YOUR RIGHTS

When debt collectors come knocking, it can feel overwhelming. But knowing your rights can transform this experience from intimidating to manageable. The Fair Debt Collection Practices Act (FD CPA) is there to protect you from abusive practices. This law prohibits debt collectors from engaging in harassment, lying, or using unfair methods to collect a debt. They can't call you at inconvenient times, like before 8 a.m. or after 9 p.m., nor can they contact you at work if they've been told not to. They must also provide a written notice detailing the amount you owe, the name of the creditor, and a statement of your right to dispute the debt within 30 days. Understanding these provisions can empower you to stand firm and ensure your rights are respected.

Effective communication with collectors is key to navigating this process smoothly. Start by requesting all communication in writing. This provides you with a clear record and ensures that information is conveyed accurately. When discussing repayment terms, approach the conversation with a clear plan. Propose a realistic payment schedule that fits your budget, and don't hesitate to negotiate. Collectors often prefer receiving some payment over none, so they might be flexible with terms. Keep your tone professional yet firm, asserting your need for respectful and straightforward communication. This approach can help foster a more constructive dialogue, reducing the stress typically associated with these interactions.

If you find discrepancies in debt or experience harassment, knowing the dispute resolution process is crucial. Begin by filing a complaint with the Consumer Financial Protection Bureau (CFPB). Their role is to ensure that consumer financial markets work for consumers, and they can investigate your complaint. If unresolved, seek legal assistance. A lawyer specializing in consumer rights can offer guidance on the best course of action and, if necessary, represent you in court. Legal advice can be invaluable, particularly if the debt collector is violating your rights or if the debt is not yours. Taking these steps protects you and holds collectors accountable for their actions.

Documenting all interactions with debt collectors is a vital practice. Maintain a file with copies of all written correspondence, including letters and emails. For phone conversations, keep a detailed log noting the date, time, and content of each call. Include the name of the person you spoke with and any agreements made. This documentation serves as evidence should you need to dispute any claims or demonstrate harassment. It also helps you track the progress of your communications, ensuring that all parties are honoring the agreed-upon terms. By staying organized, you empower yourself with information, which is a powerful tool in managing debt effectively.

Debt management requires understanding and strategy. Knowing your rights under the FD CPA is crucial, as it provides a framework for fair treatment. Effective communication and negotiation skills can turn potentially stressful interactions into manageable discussions. If disputes arise, there are clear processes and legal avenues to explore, ensuring your rights are upheld. Documenting everything provides a safety net, offering clarity and protection. As you navigate these aspects, remember that you're not alone—resources and support are available to guide you through. Next, we'll look at how insurance plays a role in financial stability, rounding out our understanding of managing personal finances with foresight and confidence.

CHAPTER 5
NAVIGATING TAXES WITH CONFIDENCE

Taxes are a certainty of life, yet they often seem shrouded in mystery and complexity. I remember the first time I sat down to tackle my own taxes, armed with a stack of forms and a sense of trepidation. It was like staring down a puzzle, each piece critical to getting the full picture right. The experience taught me a valuable lesson: understanding taxes isn't just about compliance; it's about empowerment. When you grasp the basics, you take control of your financial narrative. This chapter is designed to guide you through the foundational aspects of tax filing, making the process less daunting and more manageable.

Understanding the various tax forms and documents is the first step in demystifying the filing process. One of the most common forms is the W-2, which you receive from your employer. This document reflects your annual earnings and the taxes withheld from your paycheck, providing the baseline for your tax filing. For those who navigate the freelance world, the 1099 form becomes familiar. This form details income received from clients, but unlike the W-2, taxes aren't withheld, leaving you responsible for estimating and paying them yourself (SOURCE 1). Additionally, don't overlook bank interest statements, which report any interest income you've earned over the year. Having all these documents organized is crucial; they form the backbone of your tax return and help ensure accuracy.

Filing status is another important component that significantly affects your tax liability. Your status determines the type of tax return you must file and influences your deductions and tax rates (SOURCE 2). If you're single, you'll file as such, but if you're married, you have the option to file jointly or separately. Married filing jointly often provides benefits, such as a higher standard deduction and lower tax rates. The head of household status is available for single individuals with dependents, offering a larger standard deduction than the single filing status. Understanding your filing status is key because it shapes your tax obligations and potential benefits, making it essential to choose correctly based on your circumstances.

Selecting the right filing method can streamline the tax-filing process. E-filing, or electronic filing, is a popular choice, providing a fast and secure way to submit your tax return. It reduces the risk of errors and speeds up the refund process, usually within a few weeks. Alternatively, some may prefer paper filing, especially if they're not comfortable with technology or have a straightforward tax situation. Another option is using tax software or hiring professional services.

Tax software can guide you through the filing process step-by-step, reducing the likelihood of mistakes. Professional services, though more expensive, offer expertise and personalized guidance, making them a worthwhile investment for those with complex tax situations. The method you choose should align with your comfort level and the complexity of your taxes.

Adhering to important tax deadlines is crucial to avoid unnecessary penalties. The deadline for filing your federal tax return is typically April 15th each year. Missing this deadline can result in penalties and interest on any taxes owed. If you find yourself unable to meet the deadline, you can request an extension, which gives you until October 15th to file. However, it's important to note that an extension to file is not an extension to pay any taxes owed; you must estimate and pay any taxes by the original deadline to avoid penalties. By keeping track of these key dates and making timely submissions, you ensure compliance and maintain your financial health.

Exercise: Organize Your Tax Documents

Before diving into the filing process, gather all necessary tax documents, such as W-2s, 1099s, and bank interest statements. Create a checklist to ensure you have everything you need. Organizing your documents ahead of time simplifies the tax-filing process and minimizes the risk of errors. This proactive approach saves time and reduces stress, allowing you to tackle your taxes with confidence and accuracy.

MAXIMIZING DEDUCTIONS AND CREDITS: WHAT YOU NEED TO KNOW

Navigating deductions and credits is a pivotal part of tax planning, especially for young adults who may be filing independently for the first time. One common deduction that can significantly lighten your tax load is the student loan interest deduction. If you're paying off student loans, you're likely eligible to deduct up to $2,500 of the interest paid during the year. This deduction is an above-the-line deduction, which means it reduces your taxable income directly, even if you don't itemize deductions. It's a straightforward way to lower your tax bill if you qualify. Education-related expenses also offer potential tax benefits. If you're taking courses to strengthen your job skills or pursuing higher education, you might qualify to deduct eligible expenses. These expenses can include tuition, fees, and even course materials. Keeping track of these outlays can help you maximize your tax savings, easing the financial burden of your educational pursuits.

On the flip side, tax credits can directly reduce the amount of tax you owe, often proving more beneficial than deductions. The Earned Income Tax Credit is one such credit that can be a boon for low to moderate-income earners. It's refundable credit, meaning it can reduce your tax bill to zero and result in a refund if the credit exceeds your tax liability. This credit is particularly valuable for young adults just starting their careers. Another significant credit is the American Opportunity Credit, designed to alleviate the costs of higher education. It covers up to $2,500 of undergraduate education expenses per year for the first four years of college. Unlike the deduction, this credit can provide a dollar-for-dollar reduction in your tax bill, making it a powerful tool in your tax strategy. Both credits require meeting specific eligibility criteria, so it's crucial to review the qualifications to ensure you can benefit from them.

Understanding the distinction between deductions and credits is key to effective tax planning. Deductions reduce your taxable income, which in turn lowers the amount of tax you owe. For example, if you have $1,000 in deductions and fall into the 24% tax bracket, your tax bill decreases by $240. Credits, however, directly reduce your tax liability, making them more impactful in numerous instances. If you qualify for a $1,000 tax credit, it directly cuts $1,000 from the taxes you owe. This difference makes credits particularly attractive, especially refundable ones that can result in a refund if they exceed your total tax bill. Strategic planning involves understanding how to leverage both deductions and credits to your advantage, optimizing your tax situation. Knowing how each affects your overall tax bill allows you to plan more effectively, ensuring you maximize the benefits available to you.

To claim these benefits, meticulous documentation is essential. Keeping accurate records of your expenses and income is not just a best practice but a necessity. Receipts and invoices are your proof of eligible deductions and credits, serving as a safeguard if the IRS questions your claims. For education-related deductions or credits, maintaining copies of tuition statements, proof of payment, and educational transcripts is crucial. These documents substantiate your eligibility and prevent disputes with tax authorities. Organization is key—consider using digital tools to scan and store documents, ensuring easy access when needed. By staying diligent in your record-keeping, you make the tax-filing process smoother and protect yourself from potential audits or discrepancies. This proactive approach simplifies your tax preparation and ensures you can confidently claim the deductions and credits you're entitled to.

UNDERSTANDING YOUR TAX BRACKET: WHAT IT MEANS FOR YOU

Navigating the labyrinthine world of taxes begins with understanding the concept of tax brackets. In the United States, the tax system is progressive, which means the more you earn, the higher your tax rate. This system is designed to ensure that those with greater incomes contribute a proportionally larger share toward public services and infrastructure. The federal tax brackets are tiered, each with a specific range of income and a corresponding tax rate. For instance, as of the current tax year, income up to a certain amount is taxed at 10%, while higher earnings fall into brackets with rates of 12%, 22%, and beyond. This tiered structure means that only the income within each bracket is taxed at that bracket's rate. Understanding where your income falls within these brackets is crucial for effective tax planning and management.

Calculating your effective tax rate provides a clearer picture of your tax obligations beyond the surface-level understanding of tax brackets. The marginal tax rate applies to the last dollar of income earned, which often leads to confusion when assessing the true tax burden. The effective tax rate, however, offers a more comprehensive insight. It represents the average rate you pay on your total income. To calculate it, divide the total number of taxes paid by your total income and multiply by 100 to get a percentage. For example, if your total income is $50,000 and you paid $7,500 in taxes, your effective tax rate would be 15%. This calculation reveals the actual percentage of income that goes toward taxes, offering a more accurate reflection of your financial standing.

Strategically managing your tax bracket involves understanding how to optimize income and deductions. Timing income recognition is one such strategy. If you're close to the top of a tax bracket, consider deferring income, such as a year-end bonus, to the following year if possible. This can help prevent unnecessary jumps into a higher tax bracket. Another effective tactic is utilizing retirement contributions. Contributions to traditional retirement accounts, like a 401(k) or IRA, reduce your taxable income, potentially lowering your marginal tax rate. By maximizing these contributions, not only do you save for retirement, but you also reduce your current tax liability. This dual benefit makes retirement contributions a powerful tool in tax bracket management, aligning short-term tax savings with long-term financial goals.

Life changes often bring about shifts in tax brackets, requiring adjustments to your tax strategy. Marriage is one such change, often impacting filing status and, consequently, tax liabilities. Many couples find that filing jointly provides tax advantages, such as lower rates and higher deductions, but this isn't a universal rule. In some cases, particularly where one spouse has significantly higher deductions, filing separately might be advantageous. Job changes also affect tax brackets, especially if they result in significant salary increases or decreases. Withholding adjustments may be necessary to align with your new financial situation. Updating your W-4 form with your employer ensures that the correct number of taxes is withheld from your paycheck, minimizing the risk of underpayment penalties or an unexpected tax bill. These life events underscore the importance of staying informed and proactive in managing your tax obligations, allowing you to navigate changes smoothly and maintain financial stability.

COMMON TAX MISTAKES: HOW TO AVOID THEM

When it comes to filing taxes, even the smallest slip can lead to unnecessary headaches. One of the most frequent errors is inputting an incorrect Social Security number. This small string of digits is crucial, as it's used by the IRS to identify you and process your return. A simple typo can cause delays or even rejections. Double-check this number before submitting your forms to ensure accuracy. Another common oversight is missing signatures on paper filings. This might seem trivial, but an unsigned form is considered incomplete and will be returned for correction. Always verify that all required signatures are in place before you send your return. These checks, though seemingly minor, play a vital role in ensuring a smooth filing process, helping you avoid delays and potential penalties.

Differentiating between taxable and non-taxable income is another area where many taxpayers stumble. Not all income is created equal according to the IRS. For instance, gifts and inheritances are generally not subject to income tax, making them non-taxable. However, if these gifts generate income, such as interest or dividends, that income is taxable. On the other hand, tax-exempt interest, often earned from certain municipal bonds, is not subject to federal taxes. Understanding these distinctions helps prevent reporting errors that could lead to audits or fines. Knowing what needs to be included in your taxable income—and what doesn't—simplifies the filing process and ensures compliance with tax laws. It's about having a clear picture of where you stand financially and reporting accurately to avoid complications.

Another pitfall is overlooking available deductions and credits. Moving expenses for job relocation, though now limited to active-duty military members, were once a common deduction often missed by those eligible. Similarly, the retirement savings contributions credit can reduce your tax liability if you've contributed to qualified retirement plans. This credit is particularly beneficial for those with moderate incomes, encouraging savings for the future while providing immediate tax relief. Overlooking these opportunities means potentially paying more than necessary. To avoid this, familiarize yourself with the deductions and credits applicable to your situation.

Stay informed about tax changes each year to ensure you claim everything you're entitled to, maximizing your tax benefits and minimizing your liabilities. Being proactive and thorough in this area can lead to substantial savings.

Ensuring complete and accurate tax returns is essential for avoiding issues with the IRS. Reviewing all entries on your return is a simple yet effective way to catch mistakes. Look for errors in calculations, overlooked income, or incorrect deduction amounts. It's easy to miss a detail when you're working through pages of figures, but a careful review can save you from costly errors. Using software validation features can also help. Many tax preparation programs have built-in checks that flag potential mistakes, guiding you to areas that need attention. These tools provide an extra layer of security, helping ensure that your return is accurate before submission. Taking the time to thoroughly review your return is a worthwhile investment, reducing the risk of audits and ensuring you receive any refunds promptly. A meticulous approach to your tax preparation can result in a stress-free filing experience and peace of mind.

TAX PLANNING THROUGHOUT THE YEAR: STAYING PREPARED

Getting a grip on taxes isn't just a once-a-year event; it's a year-round commitment that can save you both time and money when tax season rolls around. One of the simplest yet most effective tools at your disposal is a tax calendar. This personal planner helps you keep track of key dates and tasks, such as when quarterly estimated tax payments are due. For freelancers or those with additional income sources, these quarterly payments are critical to avoiding underpayment penalties. Instead of scrambling at the last minute, mark these dates well in advance. Alongside these quarterly tasks, year-end planning deadlines should also find a place in your calendar. These are the moments to review your financial year, assess your income, and make strategic decisions to optimize your taxes. By making a habit of checking your calendar, you stay proactive, not reactive, about your tax obligations.

Adjusting your withholding and estimated payments is another piece of the tax planning puzzle. The W-4 form is your go-to tool for adjusting how much tax is withheld from your paycheck. This form is typically filled out when you start a new job, but it's wise to revisit it whenever your financial situation changes. A life event like marriage or a new job can alter your tax needs, necessitating an update to your withholding allowances. Calculating quarterly tax estimates is equally important, especially for self-employed individuals. This involves estimating your expected income and taxes for the year and dividing this figure by four to determine your quarterly payments. By ensuring your estimated payments are accurate, you mitigate the risk of an unexpected tax bill come April. This proactive approach keeps you on top of your finances, allowing you to manage your cash flow effectively and avoid surprises.

Year-round record keeping is the unsung hero of tax preparation. Maintaining organized records throughout the year reduces the stress of hunting for documents at tax time. Start by categorizing your expenses into relevant categories, such as business, education, or medical. This organization makes it easier to identify deductible expenses and ensures you don't miss out on any tax-saving opportunities. Digital storage solutions can be a lifesaver here. Use apps or cloud-based storage to keep digital copies of receipts, invoices, and other important documents. This declutters your physical space and provides easy access to your records whenever you need them. Regularly updating and reviewing these records ensures that when tax season arrives, you're prepared and confident, not scrambling for misplaced paperwork.

As the year winds down, it's time to employ effective end-of-year tax strategies. One such strategy is making charitable contributions, which can provide a meaningful tax deduction while also supporting causes you care about. Ensure that you keep receipts and documentation for these contributions, as they are necessary for claiming deductions. Another tactic is harvesting tax losses, which involves selling investments that have declined in value to offset gains elsewhere in your portfolio. This strategy can help reduce your taxable income, thus lowering your tax liability. However, be aware of the wash-sale rule, which prevents you from buying the same or substantially identical security within 30 days. By planning these moves before the year's end, you can position yourself for a more favorable tax outcome. This strategic foresight maximizes your deductions and credits and aligns your financial planning with your long-term goals.

THE GIG ECONOMY AND TAXES: REPORTING SIDE INCOME

Recently, the gig economy has transformed how people earn a living, offering flexibility and autonomy. However, with these benefits come specific tax obligations that gig workers must navigate. As a participant in this economy, it's important to understand that you are generally considered self-employed. This classification carries the responsibility of paying self-employment tax in addition to income tax. The self-employment tax covers your contributions to Social Security and Medicare, which are typically withheld by an employer in a traditional job setting. Without an employer, you must calculate and remit these taxes yourself, which requires a proactive approach to financial planning. Additionally, you're required to report all income sources, whether you receive a 1099 form or not, as the IRS expects you to declare all earnings, even those paid in cash or through non-traditional means.

Keeping track of income and expenses is paramount to managing your tax obligations effectively. The nature of gig work often results in income from multiple sources, which can be challenging to track without a system in place. Using spreadsheets or tracking apps can simplify this task, providing a centralized location to record every transaction. These tools help ensure that nothing slips through the cracks, offering clarity and accuracy when it's time to file taxes. Alongside income tracking, it's essential to document deductible business expenses meticulously. Common deductions include mileage for work-related travel, office supplies, and equipment necessary for your services. These deductions can significantly reduce your taxable income, thus lowering your overall tax bill. By maintaining detailed records, you maximize your deductions and create a robust defense in case of an audit.

For those in the gig economy, making quarterly tax payments is a critical practice to avoid penalties. Since taxes aren't withheld from your earnings, it's your responsibility to pay estimated taxes quarterly. To calculate these payments, estimate your annual income and tax liability, then divide this figure into four equal payments. The IRS provides forms and instructions to guide you through this process, ensuring you remain compliant with tax laws. Submitting payments on time is crucial, as late payments can result in penalties and interest charges. By planning ahead and setting aside a portion of your earnings regularly, you can meet these obligations without financial strain. Staying on top of these quarterly payments not only keeps you in good standing with the IRS but also helps you manage your cash flow throughout the year.

Unique tax considerations for gig workers go beyond what traditional employees might encounter. One such consideration is the home office deduction, which can offer significant tax savings if you use part of your home exclusively for work. To qualify, this space must be your principal place of business or where you regularly meet clients. The IRS allows you to calculate this deduction using the simplified method or actual expenses, giving you flexibility in how you claim it. Handling 1099 forms from clients also requires attention. These forms report the income paid to you, but it's crucial to track your earnings independently, as discrepancies can occur. Keeping your records aligned with what clients report ensures that your tax return accurately reflects your income, preventing potential issues with the IRS.

The gig economy offers a wealth of opportunities, but it also demands careful financial management. By understanding your tax obligations, tracking income and expenses diligently, and making timely tax payments, you can navigate this landscape with confidence. These practices help you fulfill your tax responsibilities and empower you to maximize your earnings and maintain financial stability in an ever-evolving economic environment. As you continue to explore the gig economy, remember that proactive tax management is a cornerstone of success, enabling you to focus on what you do best while staying compliant with the law.

CHAPTER 6
EXPLORING ENTREPRENEURSHIP AND SIDE HUSTLES

Imagine standing at the crossroads of creativity and opportunity, where your unique skills and passions converge into a path of entrepreneurship. This chapter invites you to explore the exciting world of side hustles, an adventure where your talents can blossom into profitable ventures. The idea of turning a passion into a source of income is no longer a distant dream but a tangible reality. Whether you're a student yearning for extra cash, a professional seeking fulfillment beyond the 9-to-5, or someone eager to test the waters of business ownership, the journey begins with recognizing what you offer. It's about discovering the hidden talents and interests that can transform your financial landscape.

IDENTIFYING YOUR SKILLS: FINDING PROFITABLE OPPORTUNITIES

The first step in this entrepreneurial journey is conducting a skills inventory. This isn't just a list of what you're good at; it's a deep dive into your personal skills and hobbies that could translate into business opportunities. Begin by considering the activities that engage you most. Are you a tech enthusiast who can fix almost anything? Perhaps you have an eye for design or a knack for writing compelling stories. These skills can be the foundation of a profitable side hustle. Think about experiences and achievements that highlight your capabilities. Maybe you've been the go-to person for organizing events or have led successful projects at work. These experiences reveal your strengths and spark ideas for potential business ventures. This inventory is not just a list; it's a reflection of your unique value proposition in the marketplace (SOURCE 1).

Once you've identified your skills, the next step is researching market demand. Understanding where your skills fit into the current economic landscape is crucial. Start by conducting online surveys and polls to gauge interest in your offerings. Social media platforms can be valuable tools for gathering feedback on potential ideas. Competitor analysis is another essential component. Look at businesses offering similar services or products. What are they doing well, and where are their gaps? This analysis helps you identify opportunities to differentiate your offerings and find your niche. By understanding the competitive landscape, you can position yourself strategically to meet market needs. It's about aligning your skills with what people are willing to pay for, creating a business idea that resonates with potential customers.

Matching your skills with market needs involves identifying underserved markets where your talents can fill a gap. Consider areas where consumers are dissatisfied with existing options or where demand exceeds supply. Leveraging unique talents can set you apart from competitors. Perhaps you offer a personalized touch or have a unique perspective that others lack. These differentiators can be your selling points, attracting customers who value what you bring to the table. Finding this alignment between skills and market demand is the essence of a viable business idea. It's about seeing where you fit in the bigger picture and how you can offer something truly valuable to your audience.

Exploring various income streams based on your identified skills opens up a world of possibilities. Freelancing platforms like Upwork and Fiverr (SOURCE 2) provide avenues for offering your services to a global audience. Whether it's graphic design, writing, or coding, these platforms connect you with clients seeking your expertise. Alternatively, if your skills lie in crafting or creating unique products, platforms like Etsy allow you to reach customers who appreciate handmade goods. These income streams diversify your earnings and provide flexibility in how you work. They enable you to test different markets and refine your offerings, learning what works best for you. The key is to remain open to exploring new opportunities and adapting your approach as you gain insights.

Exercise: Skills Inventory and Market Research

Take some time to list your personal skills and hobbies. Reflect on experiences and achievements that highlight your strengths. Next, research the market demand for each skill. Consider conducting online surveys or browsing freelancing platforms to understand potential opportunities. Note any underserved markets or areas where your talents can make an impact. This exercise will help you identify and refine your business idea, setting the stage for a successful side hustle.

STARTING A SIDE HUSTLE: FROM IDEA TO INCOME

Kicking off a side hustle begins with crafting a solid business plan. Think of this plan as your roadmap, guiding you through the initial stages of your venture. At the heart of your plan are SMART goals, specific, measurable, attainable, relevant, and time-bound objectives that provide clarity and focus. These goals anchor your efforts and give you a clear path forward. Next, identify your target market. Who are the people most likely to benefit from your product or service? Develop detailed customer profiles to understand their needs, preferences, and behaviors. This insight is vital in tailoring your offerings to meet market demand effectively. Financial projections also play a crucial role in your business plan, offering a forecast of your expected earnings and expenses. These projections help you gauge the viability of your side hustle and set realistic expectations for growth. With a robust business plan in hand, you're better equipped to navigate the challenges of entrepreneurship and steer your side hustle toward success.

Once your plan is in place, focus on the initial setup and branding of your side hustle. A unique business name is the first step in creating a memorable brand identity. Choose a name that reflects your mission and resonates with your target audience. It should be easy to remember, pronounce, and spell, ensuring it sticks in the minds of potential customers. Alongside your business name, design a simple yet impactful logo. This visual representation of your brand should be versatile enough to work across various mediums, from business cards to social media profiles. An effective logo captures the essence of your brand and sets you apart from competitors. As you build your online presence, consider creating a website or social media profiles to showcase your offerings. These platforms serve as your digital storefront, providing a space for customers to learn more about your products or services and engage with your brand. A strong online presence enhances your credibility and makes it easier for potential customers to find and connect with you.

Launching your side hustle requires strategic planning and execution to reach your initial customers. Leverage social media as a powerful tool to promote your business and engage with your audience. Platforms like Instagram, Facebook, and LinkedIn offer diverse opportunities to showcase your offerings through posts, stories, and ads. Share engaging content that highlights the value of your products or services, and interact with your followers to build a community around your brand. Consider initiating a soft launch, which involves introducing your side hustle to a smaller audience before a full-scale launch. This approach allows you to test your offerings, gather feedback, and make necessary adjustments without the pressure of a large-scale debut. A soft launch provides valuable insights into customer perceptions and uncovers areas for improvement, ensuring your official launch is as polished and impactful as possible.

Tracking your side hustle's early progress is crucial for identifying areas of success and opportunities for improvement. Monitor key performance indicators (KPIs) to assess your business's performance against your goals. Are you meeting your sales targets? Is customer engagement where you want it to be? Gathering customer feedback is another essential component of this process. Encourage your customers to share their experiences and suggestions, whether through surveys, reviews, or direct communication. This feedback offers invaluable insights into what works and what needs refinement. Based on this information, be open to pivoting your approach. If certain aspects of your business aren't resonating with customers, don't hesitate to make changes. Whether it's adjusting pricing, enhancing product features, or refining your marketing strategy, flexibility and adaptability are key to maintaining momentum and ensuring your side hustle's ongoing success. As you continue to iterate and improve, you'll strengthen your business and build a loyal customer base that supports your growth.

BALANCING A SIDE HUSTLE WITH WORK OR SCHOOL

Finding the right balance between your main job or academic commitments and a side hustle can be challenging, yet immensely rewarding. Effective time management is the cornerstone of success in juggling these responsibilities. Start by creating a daily schedule that accommodates all your duties. It's not just about blocking out time; it's about prioritizing tasks to maximize productivity. One useful tool is the Eisenhower Box, a method that helps you categorize tasks based on urgency and importance. By distinguishing between what needs immediate attention and what can be deferred, you streamline your day and ensure that essential tasks receive the focus they deserve. This strategic approach prevents you from feeling overwhelmed and helps maintain a steady momentum in both your primary responsibilities and your side hustle.

Setting boundaries is equally important in maintaining a healthy work-life balance. Without clear boundaries, it's easy to let one area of your life spill over into another, leading to burnout. Allocate specific hours dedicated solely to your side hustle. This helps you stay organized and ensures that you have time to recharge and engage in personal activities. Communicating your availability to clients is another critical aspect. Let them know when you are and aren't reachable, setting realistic expectations for response times. This transparency fosters respect and understanding, allowing you to manage client relationships effectively without sacrificing other commitments. By establishing these boundaries, you create a structure that supports your well-being and productivity.

In today's digital age, utilizing productivity tools can significantly enhance your efficiency. Project management software like Trello or Asana offers a platform to organize tasks, set deadlines, and track progress. These tools provide a visual overview of your workload, helping you manage multiple projects seamlessly. Time-tracking apps are also beneficial. They allow you to monitor how much time you spend on various tasks, offering insights into your work habits and helping identify areas for improvement. By understanding where your time goes, you can make informed decisions about how to allocate it more effectively. Embracing these technologies streamlines your workflow and empowers you to achieve more in less time.

Building a support system is another key element in balancing your commitments. Surround yourself with people who understand and encourage your entrepreneurial pursuits. Sharing your goals with a mentor can provide valuable guidance and perspective, helping you navigate challenges with greater confidence. This relationship offers not only accountability but also inspiration and advice from someone who has walked a similar path. Lean on family and friends for encouragement during tough times. Their support can be a source of strength, reminding you why you started your side hustle in the first place. A strong support system acts as a safety net, providing emotional and practical assistance when needed.

Reflection: Your Balance Strategy

Reflect on your current approach to balancing a side hustle with other responsibilities. Are there areas where you struggle to maintain equilibrium? Consider implementing some of the strategies discussed, such as creating a structured schedule or utilizing productivity tools. Write down your thoughts and identify one or two changes you can make to improve your balance. This reflection is an opportunity to reassess your priorities and ensure that your side hustle enhances rather than detracts from your overall quality of life.

LEGAL CONSIDERATIONS FOR ENTREPRENEURS: STAYING COMPLIANT

Understanding the legal landscape is crucial when launching any entrepreneurial venture. The choice of business structure fundamentally affects both your liability and your tax obligations. A sole proprietorship is the simplest form, where you and the business are legally the same entity. It offers ease of setup and minimal regulatory hurdles but comes with unlimited personal liability. This means that if your business incurs debt or legal issues, your personal assets could be at risk. On the other hand, forming a Limited Liability Company (LLC) provides a layer of protection by distinguishing personal assets from business liabilities. It's a bit more complex to establish, but it offers peace of mind by safeguarding your personal finances. Tax implications also vary between these structures.

Sole proprietors report business income on their personal tax returns, while LLCs have flexibility, allowing taxation as a sole proprietorship, partnership, or corporation, depending on what suits the business best.

Once you decide on a structure, the next step is registering your business. This process begins with choosing a unique business name that reflects your brand and checking its availability. You'll need to register this name with the appropriate state authorities, ensuring it complies with all local regulations. If you're opting for an LLC, you'll likely need to file articles of organization. Following this, obtaining an Employer Identification Number (EIN) from the IRS is essential. This number acts like a social security number for your business, allowing you to open a business bank account, hire employees, and file taxes. Some states also require you to register for state-level taxes or obtain specific permits or licenses, depending on your business activities. These steps may seem daunting, but they are critical for legally operating and setting a strong foundation for your venture.

Meeting tax obligations is an ongoing responsibility for entrepreneurs. As a business owner, you're required to file self-employment taxes, which cover Social Security and Medicare contributions. This is in addition to regular income taxes. It's important to make estimated tax payments quarterly to avoid penalties. Accurate financial record-keeping is indispensable in this regard. Maintain detailed records of income, expenses, and any deductions to ensure your tax filings are precise and comprehensive. Using accounting software can simplify this process, helping you track finances and generate necessary reports efficiently. Such diligence facilitates tax compliance and equips you with data to make informed financial decisions.

Ensuring legal compliance extends beyond taxes. Drafting clear client contracts is a fundamental practice to protect your business interests. These contracts should outline the scope of work, payment terms, and any contingencies, minimizing misunderstandings and disputes. It's wise to consult a lawyer when drafting these documents to ensure they are robust and legally sound. Additionally, adhering to consumer protection laws is vital, especially if your business involves handling sensitive customer data. Implementing data privacy regulations, like GDPR, for businesses operating in or with clients from the EU, can safeguard against breaches and build trust with your customers. Compliance in these areas shields you from legal repercussions and enhances your business's reputation, fostering customer confidence and loyalty.

SCALING YOUR SIDE HUSTLE: TURNING PASSION INTO PROFIT

Taking your side hustle to the next level involves more than just enthusiasm; it requires a careful assessment of growth potential. Start by analyzing your sales trends. Look at your revenue over the past months to identify patterns and peaks. Are there certain times of the year when sales spike, or do you notice a steady increase in demand? This data helps you understand whether your business is on an upward trajectory. Also, consider market saturation. Are there still untapped opportunities within your niche, or is the market crowded with similar offerings? Understanding where you stand can inform whether it's time to expand or refine your current approach. Assessing these elements provides a clearer picture of your hustle's capacity for growth and indicates whether the market can sustain an expanded version of your business.

Once you've determined that expansion is viable, it's time to strategize on scaling up. One effective method is hiring additional help. Whether it's bringing on freelancers for specific tasks or hiring part-time employees, additional support can increase your capacity to handle more clients or produce more products. This step allows you to focus on strategic decisions and innovation rather than getting bogged down in daily operations. Simultaneously, consider expanding your product or service offerings. Diversifying what you offer can attract a broader customer base and increase revenue streams. For example, if you're offering a service, think about complementary services that your current clients might appreciate. If you're selling products, consider variations or add-ons that enhance the customer experience. Each of these strategies contributes to building a more robust and scalable business model.

As your business grows, increasing your marketing efforts becomes crucial to reaching a larger audience. Paid advertising can be a powerful tool in this process. Platforms like Google Ads or social media ads allow you to target specific demographics, ensuring your marketing budget is spent reaching those most likely to convert into customers. Analyze your current customer base to determine which segments to target. Additionally, consider collaborating with influencers who resonate with your brand. These individuals can provide authentic endorsements of your products or services to their followers, expanding your reach organically. Influencer collaborations can be particularly effective if you're entering new markets or launching new products, as they lend credibility and introduce your brand to potential customers in a relatable way. These marketing strategies are not just about visibility; they're about creating connections with your audience and building a community around your brand.

Financial planning is the backbone of successful scaling. Growth requires resources, and securing funding is often necessary to support expansion. Start by creating a growth budget that outlines projected costs and revenue. This budget should account for increased production, marketing efforts, and any new hires. Having a clear financial plan ensures that you can sustain growth without overextending your resources. Exploring financing options is also crucial. Small business loans, for example, can provide the capital needed to invest in infrastructure or inventory. Research various lenders and loan types to find terms that align with your business goals. Other funding options might include seeking investors or venture capital, depending on your business model and growth potential. Each of these financial strategies requires careful consideration, balancing the need for resources with the ability to manage debt and maintain profitability.

OVERCOMING ENTREPRENEURIAL CHALLENGES: STAYING MOTIVATED

Embarking on an entrepreneurial endeavor is much like setting sail on uncharted waters. The excitement of the journey is often accompanied by unforeseen challenges that can test your resolve. Among the most common hurdles are cash flow issues and customer acquisition struggles. Cash flow problems can arise when the inflow of money isn't enough to cover immediate expenses, leaving you scrambling to keep the business afloat. It's a delicate balance, managing the money you have with the bills that need paying. Planning and foresight are your allies here. Setting aside a contingency fund for lean periods can provide much-needed breathing room. Customer acquisition, on the other hand, is about finding and convincing people to choose your product or service over others. This can feel daunting, especially when starting out, as it requires creativity, persistence, and often a bit of trial and error to find the right strategies that resonate with your target market. Recognizing these challenges early allows you to implement strategies to mitigate their impact, ensuring that they don't derail your progress.

Developing resilience and maintaining motivation are essential as you navigate these challenges. Resilience is the ability to bounce back from setbacks, adapting and learning rather than being defeated. One effective way to foster resilience is by setting up a reward system for milestones. Celebrating small victories along the way keeps your spirits high and reminds you of the progress you're making. It could be as simple as treating yourself to a nice dinner after reaching a sales target, or taking a day off to recharges after launching a new product. These rewards act as motivational boosts, propelling you forward with renewed energy. Equally important is practicing stress-relief techniques. Running a business can be overwhelming, so incorporating activities like meditation, exercise, or even just a quiet walk can help clear your mind and reduce stress. These practices improve your mental well-being and enhance your capacity to face challenges with a clear and focused mindset.

Failures are inevitable in any entrepreneurial venture, but they are not the end of the road. Instead, they are opportunities to learn and grow. By viewing failures as learning experiences, you can extract valuable insights that guide your future actions. Conducting post-mortem analyses after setbacks helps identify what went wrong and why. Was there a flaw in the strategy, or perhaps a misalignment with customer needs? These analyses provide a clear understanding of the issues and pave the way for better decision-making in the future. Iterating on business strategies based on these learnings is crucial. Maybe a marketing campaign didn't yield the expected results; rather than seeing it as a loss, use it as a stepping stone to refine your approach. This iterative process is the essence of innovation, leading to stronger, more resilient business models that are better equipped to succeed.

Continuous learning and improvement are cornerstones of entrepreneurial success. The business landscape is ever-evolving, and staying stagnant can quickly render your efforts obsolete. Embrace a mindset of lifelong learning by attending workshops and seminars. These events offer fresh perspectives and new skills, enhancing your ability to adapt to changing market dynamics. Additionally, joining entrepreneur groups and forums can be incredibly beneficial. These communities provide a platform for sharing experiences, seeking advice, and learning from the successes and failures of others. They foster a sense of camaraderie, reminding you that you're not alone in your entrepreneurial journey. Engaging with such groups keeps you abreast of industry trends and innovations, equipping you with the knowledge needed to stay ahead of the curve.

This chapter has explored the multifaceted challenges of entrepreneurship and provided strategies to stay motivated and resilient. As you continue on this path, remember that each challenge is an opportunity for growth, shaping you into a more adept and confident entrepreneur. In the next chapter, we'll delve into the realm of insurance and financial protection, ensuring that your entrepreneurial endeavors are safeguarded against unforeseen risks.

CHAPTER 7
INSURANCE AND FINANCIAL PROTECTION

Imagine waking up with a sudden illness that requires immediate medical attention, only to realize you lack the funds to cover the costs. Health insurance becomes a crucial lifeline in such scenarios, protecting you from financial devastation while ensuring you receive the necessary care. Navigating the world of health insurance can be overwhelming, but understanding its core concepts empowers you to make informed decisions. At the heart of health insurance are terms like premiums, deductibles, and co-pays. Premiums are the monthly fees you pay to keep your insurance active, while deductibles are the amounts you must cover before your insurance kicks in. Co-pays, on the other hand, are fixed fees you pay for specific services, like doctor visits or prescriptions. Knowing these terms helps you anticipate costs and manage your healthcare expenses effectively.

When choosing a health insurance plan, you'll often encounter options like Health Maintenance Organizations (HMO's) and Preferred Provider Organizations (PPO's). HMO's are typically more affordable but require you to use a network of doctors and get referrals for specialists. They're great if you prefer lower out-of-pocket costs and don't mind a more structured approach to healthcare. PPO's, however, offer more flexibility, allowing you to see specialists without referrals and visit out-of-network providers, albeit at a higher cost. They suit those who value freedom in choosing their healthcare providers, even if it means paying a bit more. Understanding these differences allows you to select a plan that aligns with your healthcare needs and financial situation.

Assessing your health insurance needs is a personal process, influenced by factors like chronic conditions and the frequency of doctor visits. If you have ongoing medical concerns, a plan with lower deductibles and broader coverage might be more suitable. Frequent doctor visits necessitate a plan that minimizes co-pays and covers a wide range of services. Conversely, if you're generally healthy and rarely visit the doctor, a plan with higher deductibles and lower premiums could be more economical. Evaluating your unique healthcare requirements ensures you choose coverage that provides both peace of mind and financial protection, tailored to your lifestyle. It's a balancing act between cost and care, ensuring you are covered without overspending.

Maximizing your health insurance benefits requires a proactive approach to understanding and utilizing what's available. Preventive services, often covered at no additional cost, are a great starting point. These services include vaccinations, screenings, and annual check-ups, all designed to catch potential health issues early. Taking advantage of these benefits safeguards your health and reduces long-term medical expenses. The Explanation of Benefits (EOB) is another critical tool, detailing what your insurance covers and what you'll owe. Understanding your EOB can prevent unexpected bills and help you budget for any out-of-pocket costs. By demystifying these documents, you empower yourself to make informed healthcare decisions.

Exercise: Personal Health Insurance Assessment

Take some time to evaluate your current health insurance plan or consider your options if you're uninsured. List any chronic conditions, recent medical visits, and anticipated healthcare needs for the next year. Reflect on how well your current plan meets these needs, or explore potential plans that might offer better coverage. This exercise will guide you in choosing a plan that provides the most value and protection, ensuring you're prepared for any health-related expenses.

Recognizing the importance of health insurance is just the beginning. It's about equipping yourself with the knowledge to navigate the system with confidence, ensuring your health and finances are protected.

AUTO AND RENTERS' INSURANCE: COVERAGE BASICS

Imagine you're driving down the highway, enjoying your favorite playlist, when suddenly, a car swerves into your lane, causing a collision. It's a situation no one wants to find themselves in, yet it happens every day. This is where auto insurance steps in, offering a safety net for such unexpected events. At its core, auto insurance is a contract between you and the insurance company. You pay a premium, and in return, the company promises to help cover your losses if an accident occurs. The primary components include liability coverage, which is mandatory in most states. This covers damage you cause to others, both in terms of bodily injury and property damage. Comprehensive and collision coverage, on the other hand, are optional but highly recommended. They protect your vehicle against theft, vandalism, or damage from events like hailstorms, as well as from collisions with other vehicles or objects. Understanding these components helps you determine the level of protection you need, balancing cost with peace of mind.

Switching gears to renters' insurance, think about everything you own—from your laptop and smartphone to your clothes and furniture. Now, imagine losing it all in a fire or a burglary. Renters' insurance is designed to protect against such losses. It covers personal property, ensuring you can replace your belongings if they are damaged, stolen, or destroyed. But renters' insurance doesn't stop there. It also provides liability protection, which covers you if someone is injured in your rental home or if you accidentally damage someone else's property. This dual protection makes renters insurance a wise investment for anyone living in a rented space, offering financial security and reducing the burden of unexpected expenses.

Several factors influence the premiums you pay for both auto and renters insurance. Your driving record is a significant determinant for auto insurance. A history of accidents or traffic violations can increase your premiums, as it signals a higher risk to the insurer. Similarly, the type of vehicle you drive plays a role. High-performance or luxury cars typically cost more to insure due to their higher repair costs and theft rates. For renters insurance, your location is key. Living in areas prone to natural disasters or with high crime rates can raise your premiums. Additionally, the value of your property affects the cost. More expensive belongings require higher coverage limits, which translates to higher premiums. Understanding these factors helps you make informed decisions and potentially reduce costs by improving your driving habits or selecting safer neighborhoods.

Choosing the right coverage levels requires careful consideration of your needs and circumstances. For auto insurance, it's essential to meet your state's minimum coverage requirements, but going beyond these minimums can provide greater protection. You might consider adding optional coverage like roadside assistance or rental car reimbursement, which can be lifesavers in times of need. For renters' insurance, assess the value of your belongings to determine your coverage amount. It's wise to opt for replacement cost coverage instead of actual cash value, ensuring you receive enough to replace your items at today's prices, not their depreciated value. Optional add-ons like identity theft protection or additional liability coverage can offer extra security, depending on your lifestyle and potential risks.

Reflection: Your Insurance Coverage Needs

Take a moment to evaluate your current auto and renters' insurance policies. Consider your personal circumstances, such as the value of your vehicle, your driving history, and the worth of your personal belongings. Are your current coverage levels sufficient? Do you need additional protection or optional add-ons? Reflecting on these questions will help you tailor your insurance to fit your specific needs, providing the right balance of coverage and cost.

LIFE INSURANCE FOR YOUNG ADULTS: IS IT NECESSARY?

The thought of life insurance might seem distant, especially when you're young and just beginning your financial independence. Yet, its purpose is rooted in providing security and peace of mind for the unforeseen. Life insurance primarily serves as financial protection for your loved ones. Imagine the relief it offers, ensuring that your dependents are cared for should the unexpected happen. It covers funeral expenses, which can be a substantial burden during an already difficult time. This type of coverage is not just about preparing for the worst; it's about safeguarding those you care about from financial distress. By securing life insurance, you're ensuring that your family's financial future remains stable, even in your absence.

Two main types of life insurance policies cater to different needs and financial situations: term life insurance and whole life insurance. Term life insurance is straightforward, offering coverage for a specific period, such as 10, 20, or 30 years. It's often the more affordable option, making it appealing to young adults who are just starting out. If you outlive the term, the policy simply expires, but during the term, it provides peace of mind with substantial coverage at a relatively low cost. On the other hand, whole life insurance is more complex. It provides lifelong coverage and includes a savings component known as cash value, which grows over time. While whole life insurance tends to be more expensive, it offers the dual benefit of insurance protection and an investment-like savings account. Choosing between these types depends on your long-term goals and financial responsibilities.

Determining whether life insurance is necessary for you involves assessing your current responsibilities and plans. If you have dependents, such as children or a partner who relies on your income, life insurance is a crucial safety net. It ensures that their standard of living is maintained, covering everything from daily expenses to educational costs. Even if you're single, consider your debts. Student loans, for instance, could become a burden for your family in the event of your passing. Having life insurance means these obligations won't fall on their shoulders. As you evaluate your situation, think about your future aspirations. Do you plan to start a family or buy a home? These milestones often increase the need for life insurance, as they come with greater financial commitments.

When it comes to evaluating life insurance policies, it's vital to understand the terms and conditions thoroughly. Policies vary widely, so look closely at the coverage details and what triggers a payout. Some policies might have exclusions or conditions that limit coverage. Beneficiary designations are another critical aspect. Decide who will receive the benefits and ensure these designations align with your wishes and life circumstances. Regularly review and update them as your situation changes, such as after marriage, the birth of a child, or a change in financial responsibilities. Selecting the right policy requires careful consideration and understanding of your personal and financial landscape. This decision isn't just about numbers; it's about providing a financial safety net for those who matter most.

PROTECTING YOUR ASSETS: INSURANCE FOR PEACE OF MIND

Imagine the comfort of knowing that your home and belongings are shielded from unforeseen events. Asset protection is about more than just peace of mind; it's a strategic approach to safeguarding what you've worked hard to acquire. Insurance plays a crucial role in this protection, extending a safety net over your personal and financial assets. Home insurance, for instance, not only covers the physical structure of your dwelling but also the contents within it. If a fire, theft, or natural disaster strikes, you're not left to shoulder the financial burden alone. Liability protection is another significant aspect, shielding you from lawsuits that could arise from accidents on your property. This coverage can prevent a legal mishap from turning into a personal financial crisis, offering a layer of security that goes beyond physical items.

When considering asset protection, various types of insurance can provide the necessary coverage. Umbrella insurance policies are a valuable addition, offering extra liability protection beyond the limits of your standard policies. Think of it as an overarching safeguard that kicks in when your regular coverage isn't enough, covering incidents that might otherwise lead to significant personal liability. Meanwhile, flood and earthquake insurance are specialized options designed for specific geographic and environmental risks. If you live in an area prone to such natural disasters, these policies can be invaluable. They ensure that you aren't left vulnerable to the whims of nature, providing financial recovery avenues that standard homeowner's insurance might not cover. Understanding these different insurance types allows you to tailor your coverage to your unique circumstances, ensuring comprehensive protection.

Identifying personal risk factors is a critical step in determining your insurance needs. Start by evaluating any high-value possessions you own. Items like expensive electronics, jewelry, or art collections may require additional coverage to ensure they're fully protected. Living in disaster-prone areas also necessitates a closer look at your insurance portfolio. Areas susceptible to floods, earthquakes, or hurricanes demand specific considerations to guard against these threats. Assessing these factors helps you pinpoint vulnerabilities and decide where extra insurance might be necessary. By anticipating potential risks, you're better prepared to choose policies that offer the right amount of protection, ensuring your assets are covered no matter the situation.

Creating a comprehensive protection plan involves a thorough evaluation of your current insurance coverage. Begin by examining your existing policies to understand what they cover and where they might fall short. Are there gaps in your coverage that could leave you exposed? Identifying these gaps is essential for building a robust protection strategy. Consider consulting an insurance advisor to gain insights into potential areas of improvement. They can help you navigate complex policy details and recommend additional coverage options tailored to your needs. By taking a proactive approach, you can develop a protection plan that encompasses all aspects of your life, from your home and belongings to your liability exposure. This foresight ensures that you're not only prepared for the unexpected but also positioned to recover swiftly and effectively should the need arise.

Checklist: Asset Protection Planning

- Review your current home and liability insurance policies.

- List high-value possessions and ensure they are adequately covered.
- Assess personal risk factors, such as environmental threats or valuable items.
- Consider additional policies like umbrellas, flood, or earthquake insurance.
- Consult an insurance advisor for personalized recommendations.

Incorporating these steps into your financial planning can provide the peace of mind that comes with knowing you're protected. Whether it's a natural disaster or an unexpected lawsuit, having the right insurance means you're prepared to handle life's uncertainties with confidence.

NAVIGATING INSURANCE CLAIMS: TIPS FOR SUCCESS

When the unexpected happens, the last thing you want is the added stress of navigating the insurance claims process. Knowing how to file a claim effectively can make all the difference. The first step involves notifying your insurer as soon as possible. This initial contract sets the stage for your claim and ensures you adhere to any deadlines that might apply. Once you've made contact, be prepared to document every detail of the incident. This includes gathering proof of loss, such as photographs of the damage, receipts for any repairs or replacements, and police reports if applicable. The more comprehensive your documentation, the stronger your claim will be.

A successful claims process hinges on meticulous record-keeping and clear communication with your insurer. Keep a detailed log of all interactions with your insurance company, noting the date, time, and the representative you spoke with. This record can be invaluable if any disputes arise. Prompt communication is equally crucial. Respond to requests for information quickly and thoroughly. Delays or incomplete responses can slow down the process and potentially jeopardize your claim. Consider setting reminders for yourself to check emails or phone messages related to your claim, ensuring nothing falls through the cracks.

Unfortunately, not all claims are approved without issue. If you receive a denial, it's important to understand the reasons behind it. Review the denial letter carefully, paying close attention to the insurer's explanation. Sometimes, the denial might be due to missing documentation or a misunderstanding of your policy coverage. If you believe the denial was made in error, you have the right to appeal. Start by gathering any additional evidence that supports your claim and prepare a formal appeal letter. Be clear and concise, stating why you believe the decision should be reconsidered. If necessary, don't hesitate to seek assistance from a professional, such as an insurance advisor, to guide you through the appeals process.

Throughout the claims process, being informed about the status of your claim is crucial. Regular follow-ups with your insurance adjuster can provide clarity and keep your claim moving forward. Establish a timeline for expected updates and set reminders to reach out if you haven't heard back by the agreed-upon date. This proactive approach keeps you in the loop and demonstrates to the insurer that you are engaged and diligent about resolving your claim. Understanding these timelines and maintaining open lines of communication can significantly reduce the stress and uncertainty often associated with insurance claims.

Checklist: Insurance Claim Preparation

- Notify your insurer immediately after an incident.
- Collect and organize all necessary documentation (photos, receipts, reports).
- Keep a detailed log of all communications with your insurer.
- Respond promptly to requests for additional information.
- Review denial letters carefully; prepare an appeal if necessary.
- Follow up regularly with your adjuster to stay informed on claim progress.

Taking these steps can streamline the claims process, making it less daunting and more manageable. Being prepared and informed ensures that you can navigate insurance claims with confidence, securing the compensation you need to recover and move forward.

COMPARING INSURANCE POLICIES: MAKING INFORMED CHOICES

Choosing the right insurance policy can often feel like navigating a maze. There are countless options, each with its own set of terms and promises. When comparing policies, one of the first things to look at is the coverage limits. This is the maximum amount an insurance company will pay for a covered loss. It's crucial to ensure that these limits align with your needs. For example, if you're insuring a high-value home, you'll want a policy that covers the full replacement cost, not just the market value. Alongside coverage limits, examine any exclusions listed in the policy. These are specific situations or items that the policy won't cover. Understanding these can prevent unpleasant surprises when you need to make a claim. Also, consider premium costs and payment options. While a lower premium might seem attractive, it could mean higher out-of-pocket costs later. Look for a balance between affordable premiums and comprehensive coverage. Payment options can also vary, with some insurers offering discounts for annual payments instead of monthly installments. Weigh these factors carefully to find a policy that offers both protection and financial feasibility.

In today's digital age, online comparison tools have made it easier than ever to evaluate insurance policies. Websites like Policy genius or Insure.com allow you to input your details and receive quotes from multiple providers. These platforms not only show you price comparisons but also provide insights into customer reviews and ratings. Reading these reviews can offer a glimpse into the company's customer service quality and claims process efficiency. Review and rating platforms, such as Trustpilot or the Better Business Bureau, can offer additional perspectives, highlighting any recurring issues or strengths of an insurer. Utilizing these tools can streamline your decision-making process, giving you a clearer picture of what's available and what might suit your needs best.

Understanding the fine print of insurance policies is often where many people get tripped up. Policy terms and conditions can be laden with industry-specific jargon, making it hard to grasp what you're signing up for. It's important to familiarize yourself with key terms like "deductible," which is the amount you pay out-of-pocket before your insurance kicks in, or "premium," the regular payment to keep your policy active. Another term to watch out for is "rider," which refers to additional coverage you can purchase to customize your policy. Identifying hidden fees or clauses is also crucial. Some insurers might charge administrative fees or have clauses that limit payouts for certain types of claims. By understanding these elements, you can ensure that you're not caught off guard by unexpected costs or limitations.

Once you've gathered all the necessary information, it's time to decide. Start by prioritizing your coverage needs. Think about what risks you're most concerned about, and which coverages address those risks effectively. For instance, if you're in an area prone to natural disasters, a policy with robust disaster coverage should be high on your list. After identifying your priorities, balance the cost and benefits of each policy. It's tempting to opt for the cheapest option, but this could leave gaps in your coverage. Instead, look for a policy that offers the best value, providing the coverage you need at a price you can afford. Remember, the goal is to find a policy that aligns with both your protection needs and your budget.

As we reach the end of this chapter, it's clear that making informed choices about insurance involves careful consideration and research. Understanding the nuances of coverage, utilizing online resources, and interpreting complex terms are all part of the process. Equipped with these insights, you're better prepared to navigate the insurance landscape confidently. Looking ahead, we'll explore how to integrate these insurance decisions into a broader financial strategy, ensuring a holistic approach to both protection and growth.

CHAPTER 8
PLANNING FOR A SECURE RETIREMENT

Imagine standing on a sunny beach with the gentle waves lapping at your feet, a scene of tranquility and freedom. This vision is what retirement could look like—a time of peace and security. But to reach this destination, you need to start planning now. Planning for retirement isn't just about setting aside money; it's about building a future where you can enjoy life's simple pleasures without financial worry. For young adults, the journey to retirement may seem far off, but the steps you take today will shape your tomorrow. In this chapter, we'll explore essential tools and strategies to help you prepare for a secure and fulfilling retirement.

Understanding retirement accounts like 401(k)s and IRAs is crucial as they form the backbone of your retirement savings strategy. A 401(k) is a retirement savings plan offered by many employers, allowing you to contribute a portion of your salary to a tax-advantaged account. One of the greatest benefits of a 401(k) is the potential for employer matching contributions. When your employer matches your contributions, it's essentially free money added to your retirement fund, significantly boosting your savings. The contribution limits for 401(k)s are higher compared to IRAs, allowing you to save more each year. As of 2025, you can contribute up to $23,500 annually, with additional catch-up contributions available if you're over 50 (SOURCE 1). These contributions are often made pre-tax, reducing your taxable income and providing immediate tax benefits. This structure supports long-term savings and offers immediate financial advantages, making it an integral part of your retirement planning.

In contrast, Individual Retirement Accounts (IRAs) are opened independently through a broker or a bank, providing a different set of options and benefits. There are two main types of IRAs: Traditional and Roth. With a Traditional IRA, contributions may be tax-deductible, lowering your taxable income in the year you contribute. However, withdrawals during retirement are taxed as ordinary income. The Roth IRA works differently; contributions are made with after-tax dollars, so they don't reduce your current taxable income. However, the significant advantage is that withdrawals in retirement are tax-free, provided certain conditions are met. This can be particularly beneficial if you expect to be in a higher tax bracket when you retire. Both types of IRAs have their own tax implications and withdrawal rules, so understanding these can help you make an informed choice about which is best for your situation (SOURCE 1).

Comparing 401(k)s and IRAs can help you decide which fits best with your financial goals. While 401(k)s offer the advantage of higher contribution limits and potential employer matches, IRAs typically provide more flexibility in investment choices. This means you can select from a broader range of investment options, tailoring your portfolio to match your risk tolerance and financial objectives. However, both accounts have penalties for early withdrawals, typically before age 59½, unless specific conditions are met. It's crucial to weigh these factors and consider your long-term financial goals when deciding how to allocate your retirement savings. The choice between a 401(k) and an IRA often depends on your employment situation, investment preferences, and tax considerations.

Maximizing contributions to your retirement accounts is key to achieving optimal growth over time. If you're over 50, take advantage of catch-up contributions, which allow you to contribute additional funds to your retirement accounts. This can be a powerful tool for boosting your savings as you approach retirement age. Automatic payroll deductions can also play a significant role in maximizing contributions. By setting up automatic transfers from your paycheck to your retirement accounts, you ensure consistent contributions without the temptation to spend elsewhere. This strategy simplifies the savings process and helps instill discipline in your financial habits, keeping your retirement goals on track.

Reflection: Your Retirement Strategy

Take a moment to reflect on your current retirement savings strategy. Are you taking full advantage of employer matching in your 401(k)? Have you considered the tax implications of Traditional versus Roth IRAs? Jot down your thoughts and any adjustments you plan to make. This exercise will help you solidify your retirement planning strategy and ensure you're on the right path to a secure future.

SETTING RETIREMENT GOALS: PLANNING FOR THE FUTURE

As you begin thinking about retirement, envisioning the life you desire is crucial. Consider the age at which you hope to retire and the lifestyle you want to maintain. Are you dreaming of traveling the world, pursuing hobbies, or spending quality time with family? These aspirations will shape your retirement goals and help you determine the financial resources needed. It's important to acknowledge that retirement isn't a one-size-fits-all scenario. Your goals should reflect your personal desires and circumstances. Once you've painted a clear picture of your ideal retirement, you can begin to articulate specific, personalized goals. These might include the age you wish to retire and the projected living expenses you'll need to cover. It's about creating a roadmap that aligns with your vision and provides a sense of direction for your financial planning.

Estimating the amount of money needed for a comfortable

retirement involves several factors. One of the most significant considerations is the impact of inflation. Over time, the cost of living tends to rise, eroding the purchasing power of your savings. To counteract this, it's essential to plan for inflation by adjusting your savings targets accordingly. Additionally, healthcare costs in retirement can be substantial, often increasing as you age. This makes it crucial to factor in medical expenses when calculating your retirement needs. Consider researching average healthcare costs for retirees in your area to gain a realistic understanding. By accounting for these variables, you can create a more accurate estimate of the funds required to sustain your desired lifestyle throughout retirement.

Developing a comprehensive retirement savings plan is the next step in achieving your goals. Diversifying your investment options is a key strategy to ensure your savings grow over time. By spreading your investments across different asset classes, such as stocks, bonds, and real estate, you can mitigate risk and increase the potential for returns. It's also important to regularly review and adjust your savings plan to stay on track. This includes evaluating your investment performance, reassessing your risk tolerance, and making necessary adjustments to align with your evolving goals. A well-rounded plan not only focuses on accumulating wealth, but also on preserving it. By taking a proactive approach to retirement savings, you can build a solid financial foundation for the future.

Tracking your progress toward retirement goals is essential to ensure you're on the right path. Utilizing retirement savings calculators can provide valuable insights into your financial trajectory. These tools allow you to input various factors, such as your current savings, expected contributions, and desired retirement age, to project your future financial situation. Additionally, conducting annual financial check-ups can help you stay accountable and make necessary adjustments. During these reviews, assess your progress, evaluate any changes in your financial circumstances, and adjust your savings plan accordingly. This ongoing monitoring ensures that you remain focused on your goals and provides an opportunity to celebrate milestones along the way. By maintaining a vigilant eye on your progress, you can navigate the complexities of retirement planning with confidence.

Exercise: Visualizing Your Retirement

Take a moment to close your eyes and vividly imagine your ideal retirement. Where are you living, what activities fill your days, and who are you spending time with? Write down these details and reflect on how they align with your current financial plans. This exercise can help you clarify your retirement goals and motivate you to take the necessary steps to achieve them.

THE IMPORTANCE OF STARTING EARLY: TIME IS MONEY

Imagine standing at the starting line of a long race. The earlier you begin, the more ground you can cover, and this is precisely how retirement savings work. Starting early allows you to harness the power of compounding interest, which can significantly amplify your savings over time. Consider two individuals: one starts saving for retirement at age 25, the other at 35. If both save the same amount annually and earn a modest return, the person who started at 25 will have amassed far more by retirement age. This is because their money had more time to grow, with each year's interest building on the last. The principle of compound interest essentially means you earn interest on both your initial savings and the interest that accumulates each year. This growth accelerates over time, making those early contributions especially impactful.

Yet, despite these clear benefits, starting early isn't always easy. Many face barriers such as student loans, limited income, and the temptation of discretionary spending. The key is to prioritize savings. It might feel daunting, but even small contributions can add up. Begin by evaluating your expenses and identifying areas where you can cut back. Maybe it's the daily coffee run or the unused gym membership. Redirect these funds into your retirement savings. Addressing student loans while saving for retirement is another challenge. Consider refinancing options to lower monthly payments, freeing up some cash for savings. The goal is not to eliminate all fun, but to find a balance that allows you to invest in your future.

Cultivating an early savings mindset is crucial. It involves shifting your focus from short-term gratification to long-term stability. Financial literacy plays a big role here. Educate yourself about the benefits of saving and investing. Learn about different financial products and how they can help you achieve your goals. Start by setting small, achievable milestones. These could be as simple as saving a certain amount each month or reaching a specific savings balance by year's end. Celebrate these achievements to keep yourself motivated. Over time, these small steps will develop into solid habits, laying a strong foundation for your financial future.

Starting early also allows you to adopt a more aggressive investment strategy. With time on your side, you can afford to take on more risk, potentially reaping higher rewards. Younger investors can typically allocate a larger portion of their portfolios to stocks, which historically have offered higher returns than bonds or cash. As you age and your investment horizon shortens, you can gradually shift to a more conservative mix to protect your accumulated wealth. Adjusting your risk tolerance over time ensures that your investment strategy aligns with your life stage and financial objectives. This flexibility enhances growth potential and provides peace of mind, knowing that time is working in your favor.

BALANCING RETIREMENT SAVINGS WITH OTHER FINANCIAL GOALS

Life rarely allows us to focus on a single financial goal. More often, we're juggling several at once. Imagine you're dreaming of buying your first home, but at the same time, you're thinking about how to save for your child's future education. These are significant milestones that often compete with retirement savings, making it crucial to identify and prioritize these goals effectively. Homeownership represents stability and investment, while setting up an education fund for your children ensures they have opportunities without the burden of debt. Each goal holds weight, and balancing them requires a thoughtful approach. Start by listing out all your financial priorities. Determine which are most pressing and which can be scaled over time. This clarity will guide your decisions and help you allocate resources wisely.

To manage multiple goals, a practical strategy is to allocate a fixed percentage of your income to each. This might mean dedicating 10% to retirement, 5% to an education fund, and another portion to a house down payment. This method ensures each goal is progressing, albeit at different paces. Another approach is using savings buckets. Imagine dividing your savings into separate "buckets" for each goal. Physically or digitally separating these funds can help you visualize progress and maintain focus. The key is consistency. By setting aside a portion of your income regularly, you avoid the trap of putting all your resources into one area at the expense of others. This strategy promotes balanced growth of all your financial objectives.

Life is unpredictable, and circumstances can change rapidly. An increase in income provides an opportunity to boost contributions to all your goals, accelerating progress. Conversely, a decrease or unexpected expense may require scaling back temporarily. Major life events like marriage or the birth of a child often necessitate a re-evaluation of financial priorities. These moments are ideal for adjusting your savings strategy. It's important to stay flexible and adapt to these changes, ensuring your financial planning remains effective. Regular check-ins with your financial goals can help you stay aligned with your life circumstances. This adaptability guards against financial strain and keeps you on track, even when life throws you a curveball.

Fortunately, several tools can help you manage and track these goals. Budgeting software with goal-tracking features can provide a comprehensive view of your financial landscape, showing how each goal is progressing and where adjustments might be needed. Many of these tools allow you to set reminders and alert you when it's time to review or adjust your contributions. If you're overwhelmed by the complexity of balancing multiple priorities, consider consulting a financial advisor. These professionals can offer personalized advice, helping you create a strategy that considers your unique situation. They can provide insights into tax implications, investment options, and more, ensuring you're making informed decisions. Whether you're tech-savvy or prefer a more hands-on approach, these resources can simplify the process, making it easier to manage your financial goals simultaneously.

ADAPTING RETIREMENT PLANS TO LIFE CHANGES

Life is a tapestry of unforeseen events, each with the potential to shift your financial landscape dramatically. Career changes, whether voluntary or due to layoffs, can greatly impact your retirement planning. A new job might offer different benefits, like a more generous 401(k) match, or it might mean a temporary gap in contributions. Such transitions require reevaluating your retirement strategy to ensure it aligns with your new employment situation. Similarly, health issues can arise unexpectedly, affecting both your current financial obligations and future retirement needs. Whether dealing with personal health challenges or becoming a caregiver for a family member, these situations often necessitate adjustments to your savings plan. They might require reallocating funds to cover increased medical expenses or adjusting your retirement timeline to accommodate new realities. Recognizing these pivotal life events is the first step in adapting your retirement strategy to remain effective and relevant.

When significant changes occur, making strategic adjustments to your retirement plan is crucial. Begin by re-evaluating your investment allocations. This means assessing whether your current portfolio still aligns with your risk tolerance and financial goals in light of recent changes. For instance, a career shift might encourage a more conservative investment approach if your income becomes less predictable. Alternatively, you might opt for more aggressive investments if your new position promises greater financial stability. Creating contingency plans for unforeseen events is another critical element. This involves setting aside emergency funds specifically earmarked for unexpected life changes that could disrupt your retirement savings. Having a backup plan ensures you're not derailed by life's surprises and provides peace of mind knowing you're prepared for whatever comes your way.

The importance of maintaining flexibility in your retirement planning cannot be overstated. As life evolves, so too should your financial strategies. Regularly reviewing and updating your plans is essential to keeping them aligned with your current circumstances and future aspirations. This means scheduling periodic check-ins to assess your progress, evaluate any changes in your life, and adjust your retirement goals as needed. Building a financial cushion is another strategy to enhance adaptability. By setting aside additional savings beyond your regular retirement contributions, you create a buffer that allows you to absorb unexpected costs or take advantage of new opportunities without compromising your long-term goals. Flexibility in planning is not just about reacting to change but proactively positioning yourself to thrive in any situation.

During major life transitions, seeking professional advice can be invaluable. Retirement planners offer expertise and insights that can help you navigate complex financial landscapes and ensure your plans remain aligned with your goals. They can provide tailored strategies to optimize your savings, manage risks, and adjust your retirement timeline in response to life changes. Legal considerations, such as estate planning, also become increasingly important during transitions. Consulting with legal professionals can help you review and update important documents like wills, trusts, and powers of attorney to reflect your current wishes and circumstances. By leveraging professional advice, you gain access to a wealth of knowledge and support that empowers you to make informed decisions and keep your retirement plans on track.

MAKING RETIREMENT SAVING A HABIT: CONSISTENCY IS KEY

Establishing a habit of consistent saving for retirement might seem like a daunting task, but it's one of the most impactful steps you can take for your future. Imagine treating your retirement savings like a mandatory bill, something you must pay monthly without fail. This mindset shifts savings from being an optional task to a non-negotiable part of your financial routine. Setting up automatic transfers is a simple yet powerful way to achieve this. By automating your contributions, you remove the temptation to spend that money elsewhere. It ensures that you consistently invest in your future, making saving as effortless as paying your rent or utility bills. This regularity builds a strong foundation for your retirement savings, allowing you to focus on other financial goals with the peace of mind that your future is secure.

Overcoming the inertia and procrastination that often hinder retirement savings requires motivation and support. Visualizing your goals can be a highly effective technique. Picture your retirement years and the lifestyle you desire. Imagine the freedom of traveling, the comfort of a secure home, or the joy of spending time with loved ones without financial worry. These vivid images can reignite your motivation to save. Additionally, consider finding accountability partners or joining groups focused on financial goals. Sharing your plans with others creates a sense of commitment and provides encouragement. These partners can offer support, share insights, and celebrate milestones with you, turning the often solitary task of saving into a shared endeavor. This community aspect can propel you forward, helping you maintain momentum even when the initial excitement wanes.

Building discipline in saving doesn't require drastic measures; it thrives on small, consistent steps. Start with manageable contributions, even if they seem modest at first. As your financial situation improves, gradually increase these amounts. This incremental approach not only makes saving less intimidating but also more sustainable. Celebrate these small wins to stay motivated. Did you manage to save an extra $50 this month? Acknowledge it! These celebrations reinforce positive behavior and encourage you to continue. Over time, these small increases compound, significantly boosting your savings while fostering a sense of accomplishment. This strategy strengthens your financial discipline and builds confidence in your ability to manage your finances effectively.

Technology offers a wealth of tools to help maintain consistency in your retirement savings. Consider using apps that provide savings reminders and alerts, keeping your goals at the forefront of your mind. These tools can send notifications when it's time to review your savings or when you're close to reaching a milestone. Additionally, apps that track your progress offer visual representations of your financial journey. Seeing your savings grow over time can be incredibly motivating, reinforcing the importance of regular contributions. These digital tools simplify the process, making it easier to stay on track and adapt your strategy as needed. By integrating technology into your financial routine, you enhance your ability to save consistently, turning what was once a challenge into a manageable, even enjoyable, task.

As we wrap up this chapter, consider how these strategies can transform your approach to saving for retirement. Consistency, support, and incremental progress are your allies in building a secure financial future. With these tools, you're not just saving money; you're crafting a life where your dreams can thrive.

AFTERWORD

As we come to the end of our journey together, I want to take a moment to reflect on the wealth of knowledge we've explored. Throughout these chapters, we've delved into the essential skills and strategies that form the bedrock of a solid financial foundation. From mastering budgeting basics to navigating the complexities of taxes and insurance, each lesson has been carefully crafted to empower you, the young adult reader, to take control of your financial destiny.

At the heart of this book lies a vision—a vision of a generation equipped with the tools and confidence to transform their financial landscape. By understanding and implementing these key principles, you are taking a significant step towards securing a brighter, more stable future for yourself and your loved ones.

Budgeting, as we discovered, is the cornerstone of financial success. It's not just about numbers on a spreadsheet; it's about developing a mindset of discipline, awareness, and control. By tracking your income and expenses, setting clear goals, and adjusting your spending habits accordingly, you lay the groundwork for long-term prosperity.

Building credit wisely is another crucial aspect of your financial journey. Your credit score is more than just a number; it's a reflection of your financial responsibility and a key that unlocks doors to better opportunities. By understanding how credit works, monitoring your reports regularly, and using credit responsibly, you can establish a solid credit history that will serve you well for years to come.

Saving and investing strategically is where the magic of compounding comes into play. The earlier you start setting aside money and putting it to work in smart investments, the more time you give your wealth to grow. Whether it's through retirement accounts, emergency funds, or diversified portfolios, developing a habit of consistent saving and investing is one of the most powerful steps you can take towards financial independence.

Managing debt effectively is a skill that will serve you throughout your life. Student loans, in particular, can feel like a heavy burden, but with the right strategies and mindset, you can tackle them head-on. By understanding repayment options, prioritizing high-interest debts, and exploring consolidation or refinancing when appropriate, you can gradually chip away at your debt and free yourself from its weight.

Taxes may seem daunting, but with the knowledge gained from this book, you can navigate them with confidence. By staying organized, maximizing deductions and credits, and staying informed about changes in tax laws, you can ensure that you're meeting your obligations while also keeping more of your hard-earned money in your pocket.

Embracing entrepreneurship and exploring side hustles is a fantastic way to diversify your income streams and unlock new opportunities. Whether it's turning a hobby into a profitable venture or leveraging your skills in the gig economy, the world of entrepreneurship is full of potential. By starting small, staying committed, and continually learning, you can build a thriving business that supports your financial goals.

Insurance is often overlooked by young adults, but it plays a vital role in protecting your financial well-being. By understanding the different types of coverage available—from health and auto insurance to renters and life insurance—you can create a comprehensive safety net that safeguards you against unexpected setbacks.

Finally, planning for retirement may seem like a distant concern, but the earlier you start, the more time you have to build a substantial nest egg. By taking advantage of employer-sponsored plans, individual retirement accounts, and other long-term savings vehicles, you can ensure that your golden years are filled with financial security and the freedom to enjoy life on your own terms.

As I conclude this book, I want to leave you with a call to action. The knowledge you've gained is powerful, but it's only through application that true transformation occurs. I encourage you to take the first step today, whether it's creating a budget, opening a savings account, or researching investment options. Every small action you take brings you closer to your goals.

Remember, your financial education doesn't end here. The world of personal finance is constantly evolving, and there's always more to learn. Stay curious, stay engaged, and never stop seeking out new information and perspectives. By committing to lifelong learning, you'll be better equipped to adapt to changing circumstances and seize new opportunities as they arise.

On a personal note, I want to express my heartfelt belief in your ability to achieve financial freedom. As someone who has navigated the challenges of single parenthood, built a thriving accounting business, and weathered the storms of adversity, I know firsthand the power of perseverance and the importance of financial literacy. You have within you the strength, the intelligence, and the determination to create the life you desire.

Thank you for allowing me to be a part of your financial journey. It has been an honor to share my knowledge and experiences with you, and I hope that the insights and strategies in this book will serve as a catalyst for your success. Remember, you are the architect of your own financial future, and with the right tools and mindset, there's no limit to what you can achieve.

Here's to your financial independence and a lifetime of prosperity!

Corinthia Davis

BIBLIOGRAPHY

i. How To Determine Financial Needs Versus Wants - Bank rate https://www.bankrate.com/personal-finance/credit/financial-needs-vs-wants/#:~:text=The%2050%2F30%2F20%20rule,before%20discretionary%20spending%20on%20wants.

ii. The 50/30/20 Budget Rule Explained With Examples https://www.investopedia.com/ask/answers/022916/what-502030-budget-rule.asp#:~:text=The%2050%2D30%2D20%20budgetbut%20don't%20necessarily%20need

iii. How Can Partner Help Your Finances https://www.elevate.com/article/how-accountability-partner-can-help-finances

iv. How are FICO Scores Calculated? - my FICO https://www.myfico.com/credit-education/whats-in-your-credit-score#:~:text=What's%20in%20my%20FICO%C2%AE,and%20credit%20mix%20(10%25).

v. Best Credit Cards for Beginners of 2025 https://www.businessinsider.com/personal-finance/credit-cards/best-starter-credit-cards

vi. How do I dispute an error on my credit report? https://www.consumerfinance.gov/ask-cfpb/how-do-i-dispute-an-error-on-my-credit-report-en-314/

vii. 11 Credit Myths Debunked https://www.experian.com/blogs/ask-experian/credit-myths-vs-facts/

viii. An essential guide to building an emergency fund https://www.consumerfinance.gov/an-essential-guide-to-building-an-emergency-fund/

ix. 6 Best Savings Accounts of January 2025: Up to 4.5% https://www.nerdwallet.com/best/banking/savings-accounts

x. Acorns Review 2024: A Micro-Investing App For Beginners https://www.cnbc.com/select/acorns-review/

xi. Young Investors: 401(k) Savings and Compound Interest https://www.schwab.com/learn/story/young-investors-401k-savings-and-compound-interest#:~:text=Leverage%20the%20power%20of%20compound,work%20for%20you%2C%20the%20better.

xii. Tips for paying off student loans more easily https://www.consumerfinance.gov/paying-for-college/repay-student-debt/student-loan-debt-tips/

xiii. Fixed and Variable Rate Loans: Which Is Better? https://www.investopedia.com/ask/answers/07/fixed-variable.asp

xiv. Debt Avalanche vs. Debt Snowball: What's the Difference? https://www.investopedia.com/articles/personal-finance/080716/debt-avalanche-vs-debt-snowball-which-best-you.asp

xv. Fair Debt Collection Practices Act - Explore further details at www.law.cornell.edu/wex/fair_debt_collection_practices_act

xvi. The Difference Between a 1099 and a W-2 Tax Form - Turbo Tax https://turbotax.intuit.com/tax-tips/irs-tax-forms/the-difference-between-a-1099-and-a-w-2-tax-form/L8drkTeTQ#:~:text=Key%20Takeaways,clients%20with%20your%20tax%20information.

xvii. Filing Status: What It Means on Your Taxes, Types https://www.investopedia.com/terms/f/filingstatus.asp

xviii. Credits and deductions for individuals https://www.irs.gov/credits-and-deductions-for-individuals

xix. Gig economy tax center | Internal Revenue Service https://www.irs.gov/businesses/gig-economy-tax-center

xx. How to Identify Your Entrepreneurial Skills and Redefine ... https://www.ourbusinessladder.com/how-to-identify-entrepreneurial-skills-redefine-match-business/

xxi. Top freelancing platforms in 2023 https://www.linkedin.com/pulse/top-freelancing-platforms-2023-alexey-tcherniak

xxii. Starting a side business – what do you need to know? https://www.ionos.com/startupguide/get-started/start-a-side-business/?srsltid=AfmBOooGOwu5xsEn0HVxHS1qInJYhgBUN-vT9IZO_0sGyTMiTh8sAioA

xxiii. How to Scale a Business: 6 Tactics to Utilize | HBS Online https://online.hbs.edu/blog/post/how-to-scale-a-business

xxiv. Understanding Health Insurance for Young Adults https://jedfoundation.org/resource/understanding-health-insurance-for-young-adults/

xxv. Automobile Financial Responsibility Laws By State | III https://www.iii.org/automobile-financial-responsibility-laws-by-state

xxvi. The Importance of Life Insurance for Young Adults https://bs.cgcoralisle.com/life-moment/the-importance-of-life-insurance-for-young-adults-a-guide-for-millennials-and-gen-z/

xxvii. How to File an Insurance Claim: Everything You Need to … https://www.ramseysolutions.com/insurance/how-to-file-an-insurance-claim?srsltid=AfmBOorYfoZTHrnb8JxxD7uZvkOq4SlpWI75KvyEsCr9hAAi-EUI7Em8

xxviii. IRA vs. 401(k): How to Choose - NerdWallet https://www.nerdwallet.com/article/investing/ira-vs-401k-retirement-accounts#:~:text=The%20main%20difference%20between%20401,s%20allow%20higher%20annual%20contributions.

xxix. Retirement Advice for Young Adults https://firstbusiness.bank/resource-center/retirement-advice-for-young-adults/

xxx. Why Save for Retirement in Your 20s? https://www.investopedia.com/articles/personal-finance/040315/why-save-retirement-in your-20s.asp

xxxi. The Balancing Act: How to Save for Retirement Without … https://www.morganstanley.com/cs/pdf/3851393-MSVA-Balancing-Retirement-and-Competing-Priorities.pdf

www.ingramcontent.com/pod-product-compliance
Lightning Source LLC
LaVergne TN
LVHW022225200926
848481LV00006B/2123